Pattern and Ornament
in the Arts of India

Pattern and Ornament
in the Arts of India

Henry Wilson

With 223 color photographs and 89 drawings

Thames & Hudson

For

Raseel
Navin
Akash
Noor
Imaan

With all my love

First published in 2011 in hardcover in the United States of America by
Thames & Hudson Inc., 500 Fifth Avenue, New York, New York 10110
thamesandhudsonusa.com

Library of Congress Catalog Card Number 2011922627
ISBN 978-0-500-51582-2

Printed and bound in China by Toppan Leefung

CONTENTS

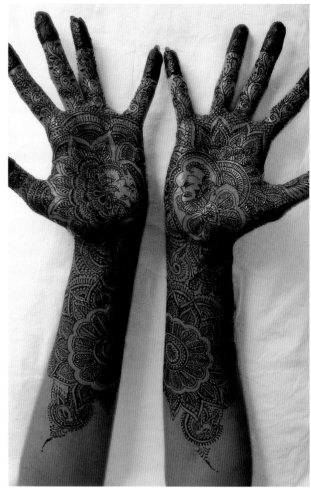

Introduction

OPPOSITE

above left Exuberant floral motifs are painted in psychedelic colours on the cabin of a cargo truck at Cochin in Kerala.

above right A bride at Baroda in Gujarat holds her hands out to dry, having just had dense floral motifs painted on them with henna. The paste will be washed off after several hours, leaving a rust-red stain that will last for several weeks.

below left A young boy at Varanasi in Uttar Pradesh dressed to play the part of Rama in a rendition of the great Hindu epic, the *Ramayana*. Sequins decorate his face, and his eyes are outlined with kohl.

below right A flower-seller at Varanasi counts out long handmade garlands of jasmine and marigold flowers, which will be used in a wedding ceremony.

Minimalism is the enemy of pattern – especially in the context of the extraordinary wealth, diversity and energy of the decorative arts of the Indian subcontinent. Decoration nourishes and ennobles us, providing physical, mental and aesthetic stimulation in a way that is inestimable. Minimalism? It disowns millennia of creative thought and action and the talents of countless generations of craftsmen and artisans. It seeks to deprive us of a spectacular bequest, one of immense variety and, above all, *joie de vivre*.

Few countries and civilizations have so consistently celebrated and practised the decorative arts, and the embellishment and ornamentation of the surface, as India. It would take many dense volumes to cover comprehensively the applied arts of India, from Neolithic cave paintings to the exuberant tailfin design on an Air India Express 737. A sophisticated iconography has criss-crossed this vast subcontinent and formed a bond between its linguistically and ethnically diverse peoples. Spreading along the trade and pilgrimage routes, it has proved an essential unifying factor in such a disparate land. With the arrival of the Mughals and their exceptional patronage of the arts, combined with their expansionist policies, there was a further development of subject-matter, taste and style.

Few physical forms exhibit the vital diversity of this inheritance as fully as architecture. As human imagination and technical innovation have evolved, so architecture developed in scope and ambition, providing an almost limitless opportunity for visual expression and innovation that challenged the craftsmen of India to think of ever more creative ways of decorating its surfaces.

The visual exploration of India's decorative genius presented here focuses on architecture – forts, palaces, *havelis* or mansions, tombs, temples and mosques. The geographical scope is restricted to north-west India, which has an exceptionally rich seam of ornamented architecture. The photographs are complemented by schematic drawings that reveal the ingenuity, dynamism and beauty of individual designs.

Three elements are essential to the evolution of this ornamentation in stone, wood, moulded and painted plaster, and glass: the natural world, the materials themselves, and the many hundreds of thousands of artists and craftsmen who have created this generous abundance of work.

Harsh climatic conditions prevail across northern India. The stark contrast between the stupefying summer months and the precious weeks of winter intensifies the exuberance of the post-monsoon season in autumn, when the landscape appears reborn. In the early period aspects of climate and nature were endowed with mystical qualities because of their seemingly arbitrary and capricious character. These manifestations were celebrated through pictorial representation, and nowhere has this been more evident than in the decoration of architecture, as artisans created a vast canon of patterns and motifs inspired by nature.

The Hindu belief system is intimately linked with the natural world. Nature is omnipresent, with its diverse and challenging landscapes, from the Himalayas to deserts and thick forests. There are the vast plains over which great rivers flow, which are the source of life for millions but also capable of being ferociously spiteful. For the Hindu population of the plains, nature was as all-encompassing for the princely ruler as for the peasant farmer. The Rajput overlords who lived a peripatetic military life were always close to nature: it is an understandable contradiction that they both exploited it and had an abiding respect for it, reproducing natural motifs in the decoration of their forts and palaces.

It is well known that the Muslim Mughals had a deep and abiding love of nature, especially that of the Kashmir Valley with its purple fields of crocuses, blossoming orchards of almonds, and a plentiful supply of water to irrigate and ornament their gardens, set against the backdrop of the snow-capped Himalayas. They worked hard to reproduce this paradise on Earth in the near-impossible conditions of the plains, surrounding their monuments with formal gardens latticed with flowing waterways to remind them of the cold streams of the Valley. In the decoration of their architecture, they froze transient nature in stone.

To their love of nature they added a passion for the abstract world of geometry. Their religion proscribed figural representation, and artists, far from being constrained, excelled in this abstract art.

And what of Buddhism and Jainism? The Buddha achieved enlightenment beneath the Bodhi tree. Few architectural structures survive from the early period, but the *toranas* or gates of the Great Stupa at Sanchi are carved with scenes of the natural environment and human interaction with it. The Jains, ascetic in ethos, built their renowned temples in isolated locations. They adhere strictly to the tenet of non-violence, to the extent that the most devout of their number do not eat root vegetables because that entails killing the entire plant.

Many Indian plants, birds and animals have acquired great symbolic meaning. On the *toranas* at Sanchi the lotus is shown as a bountiful, full-bodied flower, thick-stemmed and winding its way up the gate supports (pp. 106–7). One of the most celebrated and frequently used motifs, the lotus (p. 13) – an undisputed symbol of purity – is carved and painted in an endless variety of styles in non-Buddhist contexts as well.

It even found its way into the Quwwat ul-Islam Mosque, one of the great early Muslim monuments of Delhi (pp. 104–5).

The peacock is an important symbol for all the cultures of India: now the national bird of the Republic, it has represented beauty in all its aspects. The peacock and the turtle – which in Hindu mythology carries the world on its back – are both worked into decoration (e.g. pp. 115, 200–201).

A recurring Mughal motif is the chevron pattern, which some say symbolizes running water – an ideal for settlers in the drought-prone plains (e.g. pp. 25, 53). The rose acquired a place in Muslim symbolism: Sufi sages saw it as an embodiment of divine glory, while poets saw in it the face of the beloved. The cypress tree, a motif imported from Persia, almost invariably straight and upstanding (e.g. pp. 90–91, 199), could symbolize the 'slender, elegant stature of the beloved'.

The 'pot with overhanging leaves' and its variant, the vase of flowers, symbolized renewal, and also prosperity and well-being. For Muslims it can be traced back to the 'Tree of Life' of Persia and Mesopotamia. The motif is seen again and again (e.g. pp. 137, 154–57).

Trees, shrubs, flowers, birds and other animals cover many of the walls of Rajasthani palaces. The Sultan Mahal in Samode Palace is ornamented with one of the most joyous depictions of the abundance of nature (pp. 42–45, 230–39).

Architecture is nothing without the materials used to create it. The principal ones are wood and stone. To these are added a third, a plaster known as *arish*, and a fourth, glass. These materials, and the talent of the craftsmen, have produced some of the most thrilling architectural experiences anywhere in the world.

Wood does not withstand the ravages of time, but there is plenty of evidence for its use across the Indian subcontinent in earlier ages. In more recent times the chief centres for the use of wood as a building material and for intricate carving were the cities of Gujarat, particularly the old political and mercantile capital, Ahmedabad

OPPOSITE

above left Colour tests of fabric dye are made on strips of cotton in a block-printing workshop on the outskirts of Jaipur in Rajasthan. The brass-handled scissors are jealously guarded, used for cutting fabric only.

above right A young boy at Varanasi made up and dressed to play the part of Sita, the wife of Rama, in a performance of the *Ramayana*. He is decked with jasmine garlands and pendants and, like the boy playing Rama (p. 6), his face is decorated with sequins.

below left Detail of a new Varanasi silk brocade shawl. The design is a traditional one also known as a 'boota', a single flowering shrub motif in a cartouche shape – of a type to be met in architectural ornament as well (see e.g. p. 237) – presented as a densely packed repeat.

below right A block-printer at Jaipur uses a small block with a delicately carved iris. The fabric dye glistens on the outline of the flower.

(pp. 67, 191). The narrow streets and alleys of the old city are lined with wood-built and carved *havelis* created for merchant princes who had great wealth, power and political influence but were also deeply conservative. By the 17th century Gujarat was immensely wealthy through international trade. By then wood was no longer widely available locally, but the Gujaratis imported large quantities from southern India and from Burma.

Gujarati textiles were world-renowned; the carvers of wood printing blocks (p. 10) were highly skilled, and there is no doubt that they were also employed to work on the façades and interiors of the wealthy merchants' *havelis*.

Stone has become a symbol of eternity. The Aravali Hills that run through Rajasthan are among the oldest geological formations in the world, with rich seams of stone that have been quarried for millennia. The smooth white marble used in the 1620s for the tomb of Itimad-ud-Daula at Agra (pp. 28–33, 140–41, 199) came from Makrana, still one of Rajasthan's most famous quarries.

Stone favours the survival of architectural works of art. The Great Stupa at Sanchi, more than two thousand years old, stands out as one of the finest examples of the early use of stone as both a building material and a medium for ornamentation (pp. 107, 162). The Jain temple-builders used marble in the most exquisite and refined way: the interior of the 15th-century Chaumukha Temple at Ranakpur with its double-height pillars is like a dense white forest (p. 165).

In Rajasthan, Jaisalmer was one of the great caravanserais on the trade route between Afghanistan and Persia to the west and the heart of India to the east. The inhabitants built dazzlingly ornamented stone palaces, such as the Mandir Palace (pp. 87–88, 202–7), and grand multi-storeyed *havelis* (pp. 84–85).

Few ornamental architectural devices are more poetic than the stone *jali*. Decoration and practicality, style and function, come together in a perfect union. Instead of glass or wooden shutters, a pierced stone screen is used to fill window spaces, enabling the dwellers in the house to look out but preventing outsiders from looking in (e.g. pp. 31, 33) and allowing the passage of the slightest cooling breeze. Most have the abstract geometric patterns so favoured by the Mughals. Perhaps the best, however, are two very large screens in the most exciting arabesque style which coexist with geometric designs on a small, unpretentious building in Ahmedabad, the Sidi Sayed Mosque (pp. 209–11).

There is no doubt that with the founding of the Mughal empire a revolution occurred with regard to the use of stone as a decorative medium. Red sandstone and white marble were the principal materials used to turn dreams into physical reality. The supreme artistic and architectural achievements of the Mughals came about through a dialogue between two profoundly creative cultures and traditions, the Muslim and the Hindu: one could not have reached such heights without the other. The Mughal emperors led ambitious military campaigns, dealt with family treachery and intrigue, and were kept informed about every corner of their domain, yet they unfailingly made time for the arts. They ordered the setting up of great workshops, *karkhanas*, to train and provide work for the outstandingly talented craftsmen in their empire.

Babur, the first of the great Mughal emperors, who came to the throne in 1526, is recorded as saying: 'Another good thing in Hindustan is that it has numberless and endless workmen of every kind. For every kind of work and for every thing there is a fixed caste which has done that work or that thing from father to son till now.' He noted, 'whatever work a man took up he aimed and aspired to bring it to perfection'. Later, in commissioning new construction projects, the Emperor Akbar appreciated that the masons and other craftsmen had retained their traditional skills: their guilds simply needed some readjusting to build the new style of monument that he dreamt of. Rarely has there been such a close relationship between absolute rulers and the creative community among their subjects.

This system produced new and exciting effects, including the contrast of matt stone finishes with highly polished ones. The intricate craft of *pietra dura* – inlay with stones such as topaz, cornelian, coral, lapis lazuli, turquoise and malachite – was cultivated, reaching a standard that matched the best Italian work (see e.g. pp. 140–41, 199). The Mughals' love of flowers was expressed by their craftsmen in low relief in marble on their buildings, which blossomed with martagon lily, crown imperial, tulip and iris.

Another material used for decoration is a type of plaster known as *arish*. Current across northern India in the past, it was largely replaced in the 20th century by industrial plasters or skimmed cement, but is enjoying a revival.

This plaster is not a structural component: its main use is as a finish. It has an enduring quality and in addition it has certain marble-like properties without the latter's weight. It can be burnished with agate to a high gloss finish. In summer it has that other property of marble: it is cool to the touch. It is used to dress brick and stone to give a clean, sharp-edged finish, and for artists it has been one of their most important canvases.

Wall-paintings are found in virtually every palace across Rajasthan and Gujarat. Up to the 19th century all the pigments used came from vegetable and mineral sources and were ground and mixed by the artists themselves. This largely ended when chemical-based paints started to arrive from Europe, Germany supplying some of the earliest industrially produced colours. Mira Seth in his study of Indian painting lists colours including red ochre, yellow ochre, carbon, lime and terreverte, and lapis lazuli. 'In Rajasthan in particular', he notes, 'the basic colours were red and yellow ochres, terreverte, black and white clay along with the vegetable dye indigo. Later yellow arsenic sulphide, red cinnabar, ultramarine, emerald green, charcoal black, gold powder and foil and gum and animal glue as binding materials were regularly used.' He found an alternative source for yellow in the Shekhawati region:

cows were fed on mango leaves for a time and their urine was then distilled, leaving an intense yellow paste.

The palaces and forts of Rajasthan, particularly those of the 17th and 18th centuries, are wonderful mazes of courtyards, narrow interlinking walkways, steep staircases and hundreds of small rooms. With multiple levels, rising and falling according to the contours of hillsides on which they were often built, the palaces are organic structures growing as each successive ruler added his architectural stamp to what had been built before. From Indian miniatures it is clear that living areas were decked with portable soft furnishings in bright colours and patterns, all against the background of the permanent wall and ceiling decorations. Later buildings like Samode Palace were able to take advantage of new building materials, so interior spaces could match the scale of their European counterparts (p. 184), but the traditional footprint of the palace was retained and the walls were skimmed with the smoothest *arish* finishes.

The Rajputs are Kshatriyas, members of the warrior caste that claims divine descent, and they were not initially patrons of the arts. However, Rajput nobles were transfixed by what they saw in the Mughal seats of power in Delhi, Agra and Fatehpur Sikri, and on returning home they set up artistic schools to further their own aggrandizement. All the public rooms and many of the private chambers in the Juna Mahal in Dungarpur have a profusion of patterns, rendered in vibrant colour which retains its original freshness and intensity in interiors where small windows keep out the bleaching sunlight (p. 54). This palace remains one of Rajasthan's best-kept secrets, owned and maintained by the family but no longer inhabited.

The Junagarh Fort in Bikaner, once you have passed through the two main fortified gates, is more courtly, sophisticated, and on a larger scale, with numerous grand additions to the original building (pp. 188, 251). The paintings on *arish* in many of the apartments are among the finest in India, room after room

OPPOSITE

above left A lotus in full bloom springs out of the waters of Gaibsagar Lake at Dungarpur in Rajasthan. The lotus, rising from earth and water into air, is one of the flowers most frequently met in the applied arts because of its symbolic importance.

above right A beautifully carved stone rendition of the lotus in bud, enveloped by a dramatic spiral of stems, on the Quwwat ul-Islam mosque in Delhi.

below left A flower-seller in Varanasi measures out rose petals by weight.

below right Detail of a modern mural of lotus leaves and flowers growing out of a lake, which decorates a suite in the Shiv Niwas Palace Hotel, in the guest wing of the City Palace at Udaipur in Rajasthan.

OPPOSITE

above left Statues of Vishwakarma, presiding deity of artists and craftsmen, moulded of straw and clay, in Varanasi. The statues are made annually to celebrate the God: after several days of devotions, the family of craftsmen who had acquired a statue carry it to the Ganges, take it out in a boat, and release it in mid-stream.

above right A team of sculptors carve a marble column for a new Jain temple near Ambaji in Rajasthan.

below left Craftsmen at work on the densely carved sandstone interior of a Jain temple at Amar Sagar, a tiny village near Jaisalmer in Rajasthan. The temple is old, but the Jains have a policy of constant renewal.

below right A designer in Varanasi working on graph paper paints a dense floral pattern. The number of wood blocks required for printing will depend on the number of colours in the finished design.

decorated with a seemingly endless variety of inventive floral patterns and motifs. However, even here two rooms stand out: the Anup Mahal and the Badal Mahal. The former has dark blood-red walls exquisitely covered in delicate, intricate floral motifs brought to life in low-relief gilded gesso work (pp. 188, 248–51). With its sensuously proportioned cusped arches, inset wall niches and mirrors, and the *bangla*-roofed alcove in the centre of the back wall housing the throne, it is an intensely exotic experience. The second room is a bravura masterpiece of the imagination – an abstract evocation of the monsoon (p. 64). Stylized cloud formations in a deep blue fading to white are painted across the four walls and the ceiling. At erratic intervals gold-leaf serpents, bled red round the edges, create the illusion of lightning. In the lower half of the dado the monsoon clouds end, and the space is filled with simple parallel vertical lines, representing rain.

To create straight lines like these a string is dipped in chalk, finely crushed charcoal or vermilion powder, depending on the colour of the surface on which the line is to be drawn. Two men pull the string taut so that it hovers over the wall: one then draws it out with his other hand and lets it go, causing it to slap down and bounce off the surface, and powder from the string leaves a clear line which can be painted or chiselled out. For repeating motifs a technique called pouncing is used. A drawing is made on paper, and the lines are closely perforated with a needle; the paper is then laid on the surface, and a plump little cotton sack containing powder is gently pounded down on it, leaving a fine line on the surface to be decorated.

A comparatively recent addition to the craftsmen's assortment of materials for decoration is glass. Although glass has been made for several thousand years in India it had always been limited in its application until, in the Mughal period, it was used to spectacular effect to create mirrored rooms or *shish mahals* in the forts at Agra and Delhi. The technique for making mirror glass was imported by the Mughals from Persia: glass balls are blown and

mercury is poured into the still hot glass and swirled round so the interior surface is coated. Originally, this was done on site. Then centres grew up where the work was done in factories, for instance in Ahmedabad; but because of the highly toxic nature of mercury the factories were forced to move out, and there are now only a handful of places where these balls are made. Once the glass balls have cooled they are smashed; it is the fragments that are then used in decoration. Like so many things that are worth doing, the making of glass mosaic is a skilled craft that requires patience. (There is now a revival of the craft around Udaipur, spurred by the demands of hotels and resorts catering to tourists.) Glass at the best of times is notoriously difficult to handle, being brittle and sharp, and the mirror glass in this form is eggshell thin. The two essential tools are a diamond-headed pencil and pliers.

This Mughal innovation was an instant success, and as with so many of their decorative developments, it was taken up with gusto. Every palace across the land had to have its own *shish mahal*. As artists became more familiar with the art so they became increasingly ambitious. The sparkling effect of the mirror glass was inadvertently enhanced by the fact that the shards, having come from a sphere, were convex, increasing their reflective jewel-like quality. The Sri Niwas in the City Palace at Jaipur (pp. 38–39), the Jai Mandir in Amber Fort (p. 152) and the Shish Mahal in Samode Palace (p. 237) are thrilling examples of this decorative form. The artists in the Juna Mahal in Dungarpur took the craft a step further, painting on the back of glass, so turning glass itself into a new canvas. The Juna Mahal has two rooms that rank among the finest examples of mirrored decoration in Rajasthan (pp. 218, 223, 224, 227).

There have always been private patrons of the arts – both royal and merchant – in India. However, from the earliest days there has also been state intervention. The Emperor Ashoka in the mid-3rd century BC promulgated edicts for the establishment of schools and workshops for artists and craftsmen, and as we have seen during the Mughal period the emperors issued edicts to set up training workshops or *karkhanas*. Today the Indian state continues this tradition, in the form of the Council of Handicraft Development Corporations.

As well as state sponsorship, religion and ethics have had a guiding hand in the lives and motivation of craftsmen, often recorded in ancient treatises. The *Manasara Shilpa Shastra*, a Sanskrit architectural treatise, insists upon 'the high intellectual and moral culture necessary for a master builder. He should be conversant with all the sciences; always attentive to his work; of an unblemished character; generous, sincere, and devoid of enmity or jealousy.'

The artist was bound by the same ethics. Mira Seth notes that the *Chitralakshana* traces the origin of the art of painting to Brahma, the Hindu god of creation. Vishvakarma is the god of all arts and crafts. Jay Thakkar, writing of the carved wood *havelis* of Gujarat, tells us what the god expected: 'the craftsman seeks rhythm in his life, colour in his composition and harmony in his form, in order to perfect an object that has a function and at the same time provides visual pleasure.' The emphasis is on beauty.

Hindu artists and craftsmen traditionally worked anonymously, and very few names or signatures can be found. It was considered that their work was completed through god, for god. Certainly in the traditional crafts this remains true today. This was not the case, however, at the Mughal court. The emperors who took such a personal interest in the arts recognized talented artists, who could become personages of great import, showered with royal patronage and wealth.

Oral transmission is still the main method of instruction. Craftsmen are often illiterate but will have committed to memory all the rules their fathers taught them. The rules are based on the *shilpas*, treatises concerning the crafts. Who you worked for has never posed a problem: a Muslim can happily work for a Hindu, and vice versa. The person commissioning the work would choose the subject, but he left it to the artist or craftsman to interpret it in his own way.

When Paul Mathieu acquired his *haveli* in Udaipur it was structurally near collapse. He turned to local craftsmen to restore it and had as *gajadhara* (supervising mason) an elderly Muslim who was illiterate and yet fully conversant with all the technicalities of construction, the load-bearing capacity of stone, and many other architectural considerations. The man communicated with his charges verbally and by drawing diagrams with a stick in a patch of sand which was smoothed over repeatedly. No masterplan or written record is retained. Giles Tillotson succinctly describes the approach of such master builders as 'spontaneity based on experience'.

Craftsmen in India have always been highly organized through a system of guilds. These are very hierarchical but provide security, much as they did in medieval Europe. Among the most highly organized were those of Ahmedabad, which even had a hand in the organization of their members' private lives. The cul-de-sacs in the maze of streets and alleys in the old quarter of the city, still gated communities, were originally controlled by a specific guild and lived in by its members only. Membership was not automatic, and you could be turned out.

Even now much of India's social structure is based on the tradition of 'father to son', but nowhere more so than among workers in stone. In Agra today there are young inlay craftsmen who can trace their lineage back to ancestors who worked on the Taj Mahal. Traditionally training started early, as a child was deputed to do simple jobs in his father's craft. This is now breaking down, especially with the spread of compulsory education which exposes youngsters to a much wider spectrum of possibilities.

People in India have always travelled to where work is to be found. Craftsmen would take with them the styles and methods they had learnt in their native regions. Ideas also spread through the travels of patrons: in the mid-17th century the Jai Mandir at Amber was created for Mirza Jai

above left Detail of a lotus-inspired block-printed fabric designed by the renowned Brigitte Singh. French-born Singh is one of a small group of people who have worked hard to revive the tradition of block printing for which Jaipur and its environs were so well known. Her work is of museum quality.

above right A worker at Ahmedabad in Gujarat holds a silk screen up to the light to make any necessary slight corrections. (The pattern is transferred to the screen through a photographic process.)

below left Three women at a post-monsoon fair in the Jasdan District of Saurashtra in Gujarat. They are clothed in hand-silkscreen-printed fabrics.

below right Freshly cut chunks of sugar cane and small local roses – *gulabs*, known for their pungent scent – on a tiffin trolley in Chandni Chowk in Delhi.

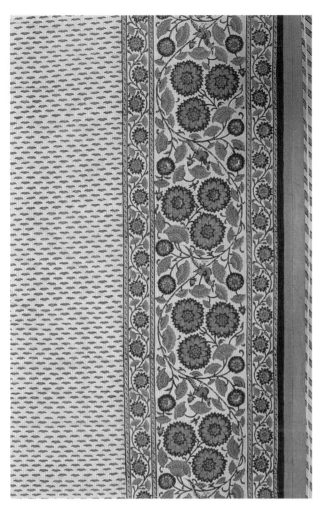

OPPOSITE

above left The chevron-patterned stone
and marble floor in the new-built
haveli of textile designer Brigitte
Singh, near Jaipur.

above right All along the riverfront of
the Narmada at Maheshwar in Madhya
Pradesh statues of the sacred Nandi
bull and Shiva *lingam* are found in
clusters or individually on the *ghats*.
The town's Hindu inhabitants use
these open-air shrines after their
sunrise ablutions in the sacred river.

below left A highly skilled stonecutter
in an Agra workshop cuts tiny pieces
of semi-precious stone which he will
inlay in a large marble plate with an
intricate floral design.

below right A detail of a Mughal-inspired
contemporary water chute in the
gardens of the Oberoi Hotel in Agra.
The deeply cut 'fishscales' cause the
water to dance and sing, shimmering
with reflected light and bubbling over
the indented surface.

Singh in a style that surely reflected
knowledge of the Mughal Red Fort
at Agra (pp. 83, 152). Multiply this
process many hundreds of times
as maharajas, princes, nobles and
officers of state returned to their
own fiefdoms, and a basic unity of
conception, if not execution, begins
to take hold.

The now deserted Mughal city
of Fatehpur Sikri, begun in 1571, is
another excellent example. This
sprawling complex of palatial
residences, offices, army housing,
elephant and horse stables and
religious buildings was created in a
phenomenally short period of time.
The immediate area, and even nearby
Agra, could not have supplied all the
skilled labour required, so more had
to be imported. Most of the decorative
work that remains today is low-relief
carving in stone (pp. 72–75, 149),
and clear stylistic variations can be
detected which can only be the result
of workers brought together from
all corners of the Emperor Akbar's
dominions.

What never fails to be exciting is
to see how from such basic materials
– stone, wood, clay and sand (in
the case of glass) – the artists and
craftsmen of India have produced the
most astonishing achievements in the
arts, crafts and architecture. Whether
it be the wood-block carver producing
an intricate design for printing, an
artist facing a wall with unblemished
arish, the mirror-glass cutter setting
out to create a new mosaic of *thekri*
work, or the stonemason bent over a
slab of stone in a dusty lane, all work
in rudimentary conditions using
simple hand tools (see e.g. pp. 14, 18).

What sustains such craftsmen?
Perhaps for the Muslim time in is
God's hands, and perhaps the Hindu
is governed by karmic law and belief
in his overseer, Lord Vishvakarma.

For many it is simply an inherited
way of life and a means to an end,
that of earning a living. A traditional
sense of purpose can still be
found in India today, in small
towns and villages particularly,
though in urban areas it has all but
evaporated as a different pace of life
replaces it. Whatever drives this
creativity, the result is a gift. The
architect Balkrishna Doshi says in
his foreword to Jay Thakkar's book
that the craftsmen 'spiritualize' the
material they work on, while Thakkar
himself writes that the Indian artist
believed that 'the true beauty in
ornamentation results from the
repose which the mind experiences
when the eye, the intellect and the
affections are satisfied due to the
absence of any wants.'

There is, luckily, a new generation
of creative minds who fully appreciate
the rich tradition that India has
inherited and which is today so
endangered. They understand that
for this extraordinarily rich legacy
to survive, it must be harnessed to
produce results equal in beauty and
quality to anything made in the
past, but relevant to today's life-styles.
The outlook is encouraging.
Designers such as Viki Sardasai with
his use of crafts including *bidri*
work and *pietra dura*, Brigitte Singh
in the field of textiles (p. 17), Munnu
Kasliwal for jewelry, and Anupam
Poddar producing functional
and decorative household items by
traditional means are, to name
but a very few, responding to the
call. As the designer Michael Aram
says, 'nothing can replace the
dexterity of a trained hand combined
with the eye that guides, nothing can
replace the hand-tooled product, an
embodiment of humanity, for such
hand-made objects vibrate with the
craftsman's soul.'

I

———

Repeat
Patterns

Repeat patterns come in an extraordinary range of styles, varying from region to region and period to period. They fall into two broad types: geometric and floral. Their adaptability makes them ideal for use on stone, mirror-glass mosaics, painted plaster, and wood. In architecture repeat patterns are most frequently employed within rectangular and square frames, but they also serve to decorate ceilings, blind doors, windows and arches, and the back walls of niches.

Such patterns frequently give an immediate indication of the patron's cultural tradition – most obviously, the use of geometric motifs for Islamic clients. The gates of Akbar's tomb at Sikandra (pp. 22–23, 25, 134–35) or the tomb of Itimad-ud-Daula at Agra (pp. 28–33) reveal a bravura use of geometric decoration and exceptional technical skill. The mathematics involved in dividing up the façade, and the endless ingenuity displayed in the patterns, are impressive indeed: frequently starting with a single unit, these geometric designs are infinite in scope.

Geometric patterns reflect the Islamic inclination to order and harmony. They are a foil to the natural world, for which Muslims had high regard, albeit in a managed and controlled form. It may well be happy coincidence that such patterns, with their multi-pointed stars, frequently have a celestial quality. They can be simple in construction or highly complex and sophisticated. In Mughal architecture they are often created in several colours of stone, such as red sandstone and white marble. Patterns carved in low relief in plain red sandstone come alive when sunlight rakes across them (pp. 26, 145). One of the most dramatic uses of geometric patterns is for *jalis* or stone screens, as in the tomb of Itimad-ud-Daula (pp. 31, 33).

Floral and organic patterns were particularly favoured by Rajput princes, who used them in their palaces (pp. 38ff.), and by the merchant community for their *havelis* (pp. 66–67), where geometric designs were rarely employed. They were most commonly rendered in paint on plaster and in mirror-glass mosaic, or, in the *havelis* of Gujarat, carved wood. The motifs may be naturalistic, or stylized. Whereas geometric repeat patterns are finished in a limited palette which accentuates their graphic quality, the floral repeat patterns in Rajput palaces have exuberant polychrome finishes. Samode Palace (pp. 42–47) and the Juna Mahal in Dungarpur (pp. 50–54) display wonderful examples of their range and energy: the Sultan Mahal ceiling in Samode Palace is, paradoxically, like a magnificent carpet of flowers (p. 45).

More often than not floral motifs are arranged in grid configurations. The grids take various forms, such as the ogee, where curving lines intersect or meet. In the Samode Haveli in Jaipur, the voids created by this arrangement are filled with Rajasthan's hundred-petalled *gulab* or rose (p. 49). The ogee format is also used in the fine plaster and mirror-glass mosaics of the Sri Niwas in the City Palace at Jaipur (p. 41). Floral repeats may be arranged in parallel bands, as on the walls of the Durbar Hall in Dungarpur (pp. 50–53) and on the carved wood façades of the merchant *havelis* of Ahmedabad in Gujarat (p. 67).

****

Repeat Patterns | 21

The main, southern, gate of the tomb of the Emperor Akbar at Sikandra, near Agra, completed in 1613 – one of the most ambitious tomb and garden projects ever undertaken by the Mughals – is noted for its remarkably exuberant façades, with bold geometric patterns given drama by the use of contrasting coloured stones (see p. 25).

above Two details of the façade of the main gate of Akbar's tomb at Sikandra (see pp. 22–23), of red sandstone inlaid with white marble and coloured stone, illustrating the variety of mathematically based abstract patterns which the Mughals, and Islam in general, are so noted for. Engaged columns at the sides are given a chevron motif, a classic Mughal design which some suggest symbolizes water.

opposite A geometric pattern from the Mughal Red Fort at Agra, where it is carved in low relief in red sandstone. In a design capable of infinite repetition, two types of eight-pointed stars contain stylized flowers, imposing order on nature.

above left A geometric pattern on the Qila-i Kuhna Mosque in the Purana Qila (old fort) in Delhi, built in 1541 by the Mughals' enemy Sher Shah. It displays intersecting circles with six-pointed stars and accompanying lozenge shapes, in lighter and darker stone inlaid in red sandstone.

above right A complex geometric pattern based on circles, on the Red Fort at Agra. These interlink optically – but not all the circles are complete. The full circles have an inner ring of lozenges like the spokes of a wheel, and an outer ring of asymmetrical hexagons. The incomplete circles have at their centre a six-pointed star containing an eight-petalled flower.

opposite This design on the Red Fort at Agra is based on staggered squares. As so often with geometric patterns, it plays games, depending on which elements the eye focuses on: it can be seen as slipping diagonally upwards or downwards, and also as a set of zigzagging tramlines.

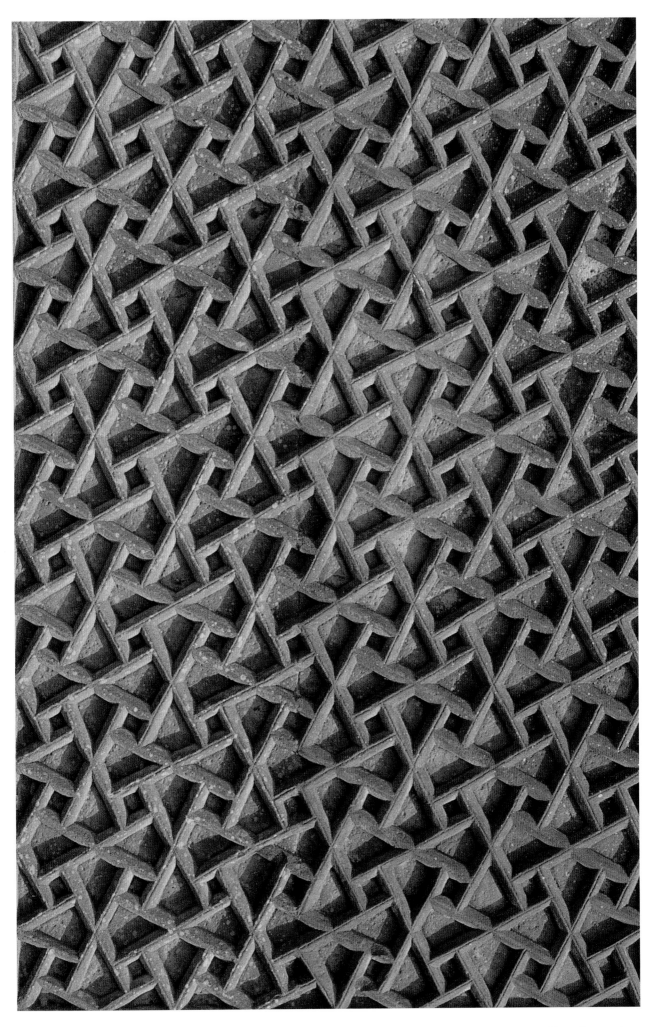

The white marble tomb of Itimad-ud-Daula
and his wife – the parents of Nur Jahan, the
powerful wife of the Emperor Jahangir.
Completed in Agra in 1628, with its intricate
coloured stone inlay it is one of the most
remarkable buildings of the Mughal period.
The entire surface is worked in *pietra dura* –
coloured stones inlaid in white marble
(see pp. 30–31, 140–41, 199). The tomb is
seen here from a gate, demonstrating the
effect that led the art historian Percy Brown
to say that 'it is like a jewel in its own casket'.

The tomb of Itimad-ud-Daula at Agra is covered with patterns in
pietra dura (see also pp. 32–33). In the dado, the linear structure with stars
and hexagons is enriched by two types of flowers, and colours
including a pale yellow sandstone and an unusual porphyry.

The tomb of Itimad-ud-Daula is exquisitely decorated with *pietra dura* inside as well as out.

above left One of the chambers in the tomb. The stone dado has a geometric pattern with a ten-pointed star surrounded by sets of five-pointed stars, framed by a border with plant motifs. The rest of the decoration is executed in paint on plaster, with flat panels and deep inset niches ornamented with floral motifs, sprigs of cherry blossom, cypress trees, vases of flowers and fruit.

above A detail of another wall with a geometric pattern similar to that of the dado but curiously irregular in its layout and colours.

left Geometric patterns are played against arabesque borders and bands on the exterior.

opposite The main chamber of the tomb. Here geometrical patterns are used for the white marble screens or *jalis*. Through them, dappled light is cast on the floor, which is covered in dramatic large-scale swirling interlacing arabesque motifs. The cenotaphs are suitably austere, but they rest on a thin slab of sandstone which has fine inlay not unlike a Persian rug.

Looking along the southern wall of the
Red Fort at Agra. The Mughal Emperor
Akbar began its rebuilding in 1564. As in
Delhi, it is known as the 'Red Fort' because it
displays the Mughals' beloved red sandstone.
The façades of one wing of the riverfront
courtyard of the Jahangiri Mahal (see pp.
142–45) – built, despite the name, by Akbar
– have a masculine, militaristic flavour, with
serried ranks of arched niches framed in
white marble. The handsome protruding
bastion displays a number of Mughal features:
the niches with pointed arches, the balcony
supported on brackets, the deep-set angled
eaves immediately above the balcony,
and at the top an elegantly proportioned
chhatri – a little kiosk with a dome supported
on columns.

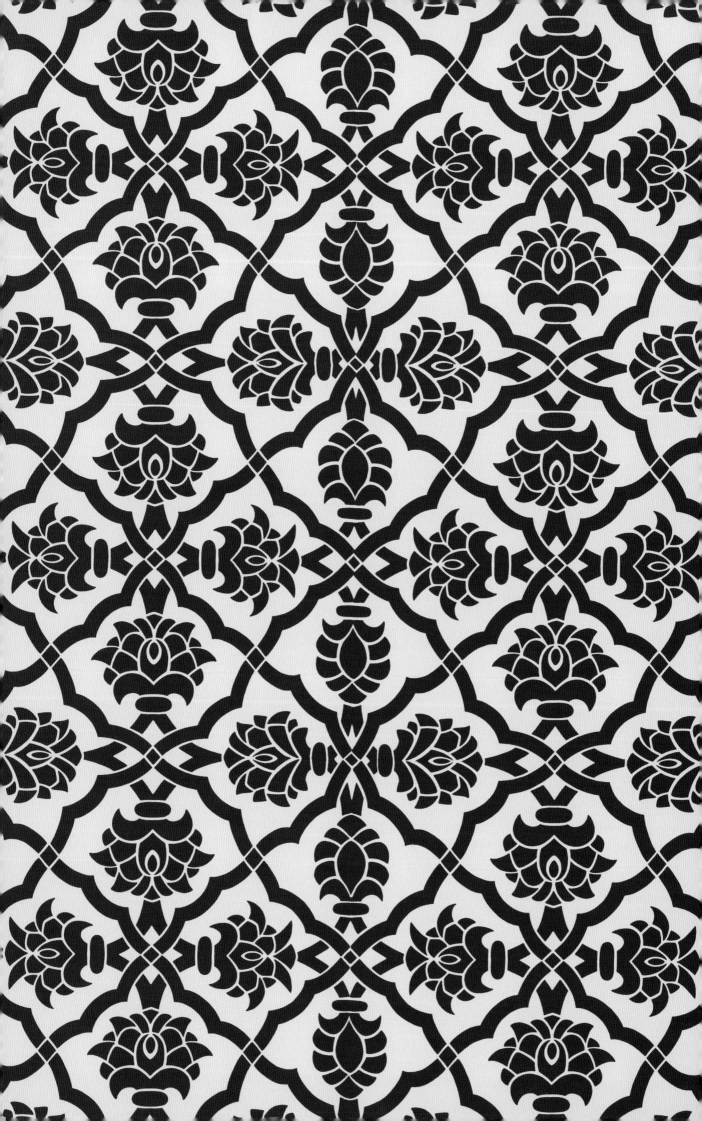

above The Anguri Bagh, or Grape Garden, and the
Khass Mahal in the Red Fort at Agra, completed in 1637 under the
Emperor Shah Jahan, seen on a misty morning. The Anguri Bagh
has the traditional *charbagh* form, divided into quarters. The central
building on the left, looking out over the garden and backing on to the
Yamuna River, was the Imperial Sleeping Pavilion.

opposite Pattern carved in low relief on a red sandstone panel in
the fort. The basic lattice is filled with floral motifs stylized
to the point of abstraction – the central ones alternately reversed
vertically, the others reversed both vertically and horizontally.

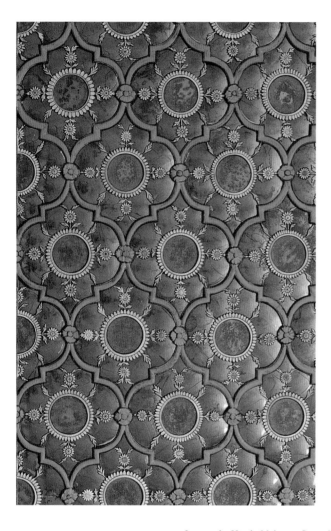

In 1727 the Hindu Maharaja Sawai Jai Singh of Amber founded a new
city in the plains, Jaipur. The great residential building at the heart of
the City Palace there is the Chandra Mahal, or Moon Pavilion; on its
sixth floor three chambers form the Sri Niwas, which is a *shish mahal*,
covered in the finest plasterwork and mirror glass.

above right and left The columns and floor of the central room are
finished in plaster polished to the gleam of marble. The ceiling is
covered with an ogee pattern in convex mirror glass set in plaster
(*above left*), while the frieze above the arcade is composed of bands of
intricate ornament (see pp. 118–19).

opposite Another design based on the ogee, on the ceiling of an adjacent
room (see p. 116). Here the pattern is as it were tied together by small
stylized flowers, while the spaces are densely filled with foliage and
flowers. The background is set with chips of mirror glass, which gleam
as the viewer walks by. Below, portraits are worked in, and in narrow
borders the mirror-glass chips are fitted like precious jewels.

In another of the chambers of the Sri Niwas at Jaipur a floral repeat
pattern is held in a bold ogee matrix with a quirky silhouette. The
sprays of flowers, set against mirror glass, are executed in plaster with
particular precision and consistency: they appear to be long-stamened
hibiscus, carnations and daisies.

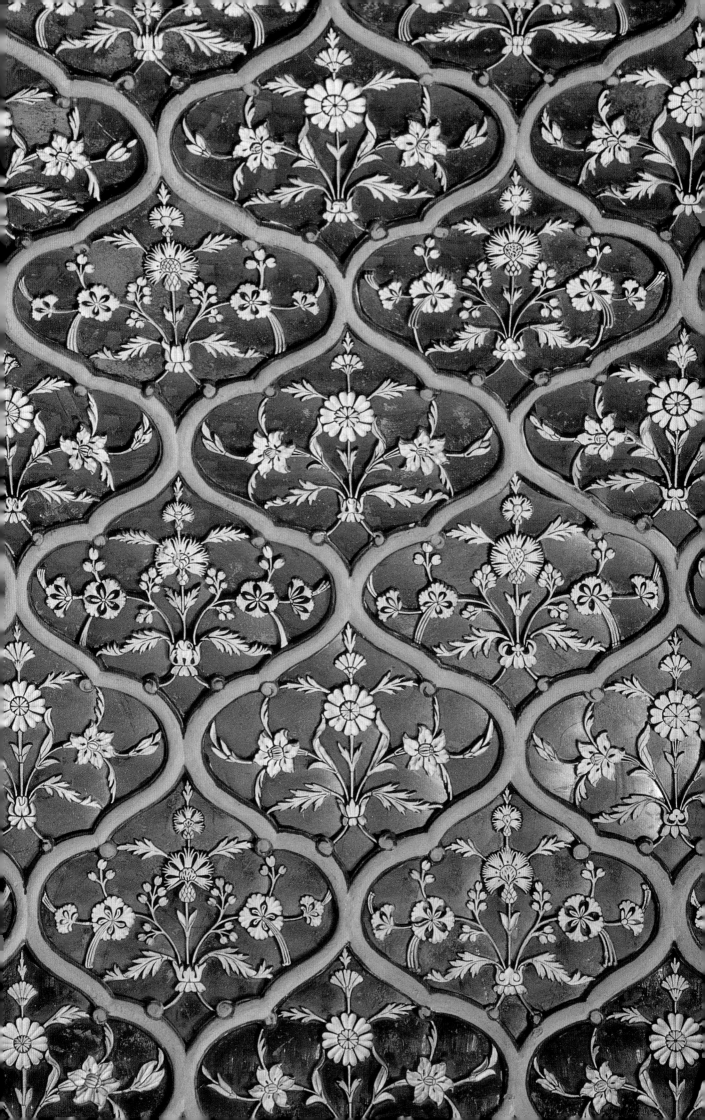

Decoration in Samode Palace in Rajasthan, chiefly carried out
for the Rajput ruler Rawal Sheo Singh in the mid-19th century.

opposite, and above left The dado of the Sultan Mahal is painted with
marigolds in black outlines and pale grey-greens. Fields of marigolds
are a frequent sight in Rajasthan, since the flowers are commonly
used to make garlands (see p. 6).

above right A passage with cusped arches runs down the side of
the Shish Mahal in the palace. At dado level the walls are painted with
figures and floral motifs, while the surfaces above are finished
with intricate mirror-glass mosaic.

opposite The painted ceiling of the Sultan Mahal in Samode Palace
is an ambitious piece of work, its polychrome finish further defined by
the clever use of contrast. It is based on a formal grid, with at
the centre of each square marigolds or dahlias, further enriched with
carnations and daisies. The stems of the flowers give lightness
and animation as they flick out in spiral formation, giving
an explosive feel to each unit.

above Drawing of part of the ceiling, showing the pattern
in monochrome.

Another floral pattern in Samode Palace, this time a mural,
again painted on plaster. Its strong ogees are linked by small
four-petalled flowers. Framed within the ogees are two types of
stylized flowers, and clearly recognizable parakeets and bulbuls.
Delicate stems form circular patterns. The principle of the
larger flowers appearing in alternating directions both vertically
and horizontally is similar to that in a much earlier carved
design in the Red Fort at Agra (p. 36).

above and opposite Roses in an ogee form the basis of this
mural decoration in what is now the dining area of the Samode Haveli
in Jaipur, the city palace of the rawals of Samode. There is a hint
of the British Arts and Crafts in the overall design, but the rose is a
small locally grown one, the hundred-petalled *gulab*, famous for its
peppery perfume (it is used to produce deliciously scented attar).

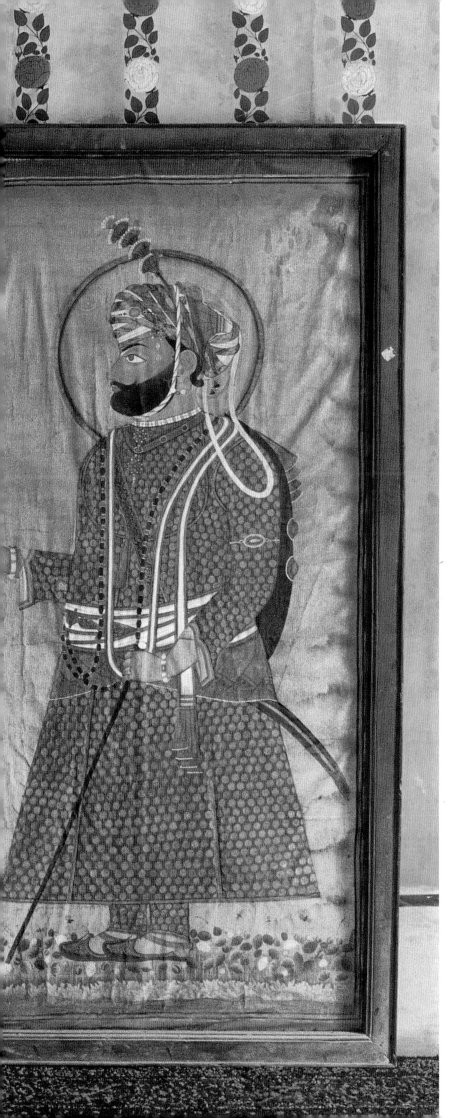

In the Durbar Hall of the Juna Mahal or Old Palace at Dungarpur in Rajasthan, portraits of former Rajput rulers are displayed against wall decoration of roses in vertical bands (see pp. 52–53).

opposite, and above The repeat pattern on a wall of the Durbar Hall of the Juna Mahal at Dungarpur (see pp. 50–51) takes the form of parallel vertical bands displaying the hundred-petalled rose in deep pink and in white, with its foliage. The pattern hints at English influence, and the wall may have been decorated as late as the early 1900s, perhaps to cover up an original mural which had deteriorated, and freshen up the Durbar Hall for an important ceremonial event.

above right Detail of the ceiling of the Durbar Hall: a simple ogee-based small-scale floral motif forms a background to bold medallions in the form of stylized lotus flowers.

right In an antechamber in the Aam Khass or private apartments of the Juna Mahal the walls are entirely decorated with a chevron motif in blue-green and red on white. The effect is to give the small room a brusque, smart masculinity, in contrast to the Durbar Hall with its vertical bands of roses. The chevron can be repeated infinitely, but here it is broken up into panels by borders of smaller chevrons. The severity of the chevrons is softened by the spandrels with floral rosettes and twirls of foliage. Inset into the wall are mirrors. (An unusual feature is the wooden cupboard doors, since wood was always rare in Rajasthan, and vulnerable to attack by white ants.)

left Part of a painted ceiling in the private apartments of the Juna Mahal at Dungarpur. An energetic, restless floral pattern serves as background to a stylized depiction of the sun. Rajputs claim to trace their origin back to the divine, and this particular image of the sun is the emblem of the house of Dungarpur. Crowned and bejewelled, it is finished in gold leaf. This heightens the contrast with the matt background, where scrolling stems wander among three types of flowers.

opposite Drawing showing how the ceiling motif can become a repeat pattern both vertically and horizontally: the original was confined by its architectural setting.

The tomb of the Mughal Emperor Akbar at Sikandra, completed in 1613, has floral decoration in the tomb chamber. (For the notable geometrical decoration on its great gateway, see pp. 22–23 and 25.) The dome is plastered and painted with a highly animated arabesque composition where tendrils playfully twist like ribbons in a breeze. The flowers are invented, as are the foliage forms. Often it seems that Mughal artists, who clearly understood the botanical aspect of their subject, took flowers apart and put them back together in entirely different and imaginary forms.

A ceiling in Bundi Palace in Rajasthan, with a floral motif set in an open ogee grid, is painted in a cool white, turquoise and dark blue palette. The drawing illustrates the dense nature of the design. The whole sits on a basic grid composed of a very thin undulating ribbon moving diagonally from left to right and right to left. This is hardly noticeable in the actual ceiling, for when colour is added the design takes on a different guise and assumes a loose ogee form: repeated pairs of semicircular shapes are held by a small six-petalled flower.

The picturesque remains of the sturdy outer fortifications of the vast complex of Amber Fort in Rajasthan. A lookout post, one of many, perches on the peak of the hill.

above left and right The Sukh Nivas in Amber Fort
(see p. 150–51) looks out across a formal garden. The back wall is
decorated with inset shapes of bowls, jars and elegant long-necked
vases (a Persian motif imported by the Mughals), painted in pastel
colours, above very shallow niches. Surrounding these motifs is a
design in low relief: this is applied as horizontal and vertical bands
and framing the hollow shapes, and also forms a repeat pattern.

opposite The design in its repeat pattern form. The base layer of the
grid consists of diamonds with points in the shape of cusped arches.
At their centres are stylized flowers, with short scrolled tendrils
that link the base to the second layer of the design. This consists of
symmetrical scrolling tendrils with paired leaves at their extremities,
one leaf extending the scroll while the other curves in the opposite
direction. Where the tendrils kiss is a stylized four-petalled flower.

The Badal Mahal, or Hall of Clouds, in the Junagarh Fort
at Bikaner in Rajasthan. The fort (see p. 188) was begun by Rai Singh
in the late 16th century, and continued to evolve until the early 20th
century. Bikaner is surrounded by the Thar Desert, known as the
'Abode of Death'. In such an arid setting, the extraordinary painting
in this room celebrates the miracle of the monsoon. At the bottom
of the walls, the storm clouds release needles of drenching rain. The
drawing shows how the monsoon clouds have been laid down in a
random acrobatic fashion. Lobes and cusps are drawn along a curve
and terminate in points at either end.

The merchants' *havelis* of Ahmedabad in Gujarat display an extraordinary wealth of decoration carved in wood (see also p. 191). These town houses are mostly raised well above street level on solid plinths, and a colonnaded veranda may run the length of the building. Bases and plinths are of stone.

above The front door of a *haveli*. The panel to the right is carved with a bold pattern of lotus flowers. The doors with metal grilles are kept closed when the house is occupied, allowing cross ventilation; when the residents are out, solid inner doors are closed and locked.

above right, and opposite A design composed of bands of stylized flowers, the larger ones based on the lotus. (Other flowers reproduced in stylized form on the façades of *havelis* are narcissus, the Asiatic tulip, jasmine, frangipani and sunflower.) Designs with such contrasting scales and repeats in vertical bands are frequently used, as well as richer compositions.

right This detail of the first floor of a mansion displays a number of characteristic features. The central element is decorated with parakeets flanking a vase. To the left a Tree of Life springs from a vase; its foliage is centred on an undulating stem with dynamic scrolling stylized leaves. Below to left and right are a pair of dancers.

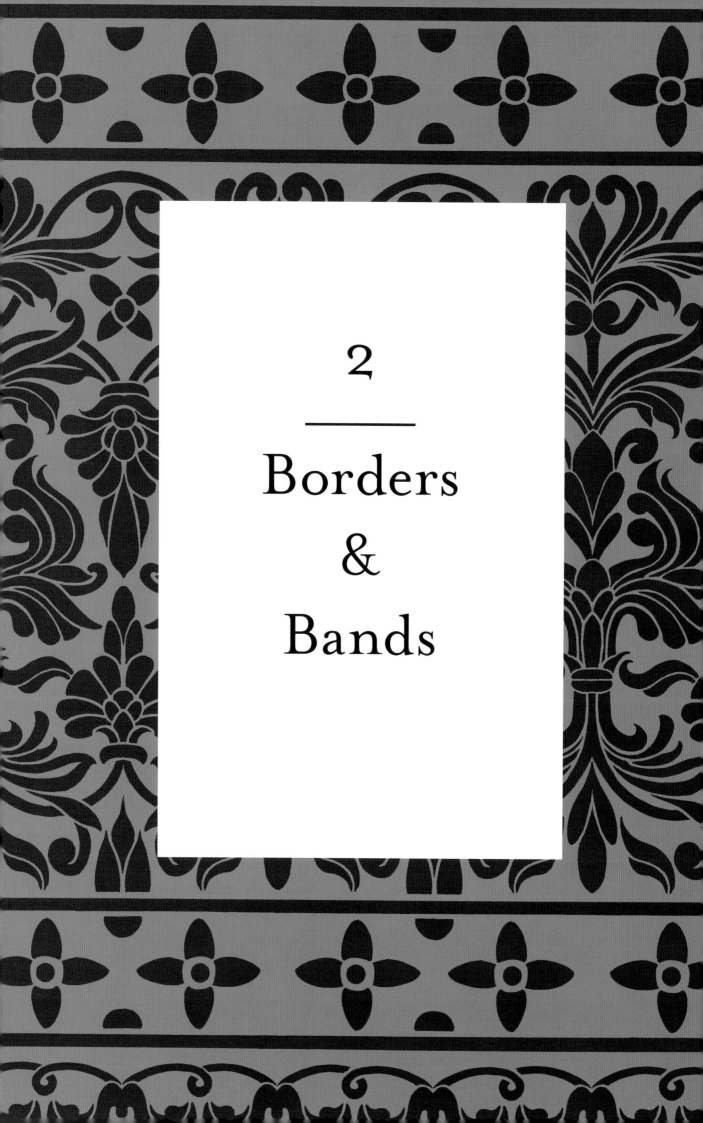

2

Borders
&
Bands

Borders and bands are an essential element of Indian architecture. They ennoble it and accentuate its elements and details. As they appear in exteriors and interiors they can be a useful dividing device, or on the contrary a link, pleasingly resolving the transition from one plane to another. They are not simply an appendage: they have a life of their own, and are an important component of the artists' design lexicon. They have a mode both functional – as a framing device for repeat patterns, single motifs and ornamental scenes – and aesthetic.

Borders and bands are spaces in their own right, with motifs that are frequently vigorous, full of movement and generous in spirit. They can include geometric designs and, more rarely, figurative motifs such as the delightful cavalcade of elephants that marches round the plinth of the Ahilyeshwar Temple at Maheshwar (p. 97). However, the overwhelming majority use floral motifs, of three types: naturalistic, stylized, and fantastic. These floral motifs are often organized in scrolls and undulating patterns. On the walls of the Udai Bilas Palace at Dungarpur in Rajasthan these patterns are combined in animated compositions where lotus motifs spring from stems: two of the designs glitter and sparkle, having been worked in painted glass mosaic (pp. 113–15).

Some borders are made up from a single unit which is repeated vertically or horizontally. In some cases, the motif may alternate in direction, as in an abstract floral design on the Red Fort at Agra (p. 76). In the border that runs along the riverfront façade of the temple at Maheshwar the motif is a playful folk-art rendition of peacocks and flowers (pp. 96–97).

Borders may also contain free-form motifs, which do not repeat but constantly evolve, like the design on one of the *toranas* of the great Buddhist stupa at Sanchi (pp. 106–7). This is a particularly notable piece of work: a sturdy, ascending wavy stem is packed tight with clusters of ravishing lotus blooms, and squeezed in among the foliage are birds and other animals. Possibly the composition is allegorical, alluding to a golden age of fecundity.

Bands can be arranged in multiples, layered one on top of the other, as seen in the Shiv Niwas in the City Palace in Udaipur (pp. 108–11) or the Sri Niwas in the City Palace in Jaipur (pp. 116, 188–89). Such layered bands lend substance and balance to the overall decorative ensemble of an interior.

Muslim floral border motifs are often more restrained and have a tendency to be naturalistic. The vertical border of pomegranates and grapes that decorates the Pavilion of the Turkish Sultana at Fatehpur Sikri (pp. 74, 75) is particularly fine. Examples of a pared-down graphic style can be seen at the Agra Red Fort, such as the marble horizontal borders of iris flowers and fig leaves and fruit (pp. 80–83).

In the predominantly Hindu Rajput palaces of Rajasthan, and the merchant *havelis* of both Rajasthan and Gujarat, floral bands run riot across and down interior walls. A frieze in Samode Haveli is packed with imagery, rich with allusion to an idealized garden, where the interlinked spirals combine with a pink climbing rose, alive with birds and butterflies (pp. 124–25).

The Mughal Emperor Akbar started work on
his new city of Fatehpur Sikri – the 'City of
Victory', named after the successful campaign
to take Gujarat – in 1571. It grew up on the
site where a Muslim mystic, Shaikh Salim,
who had successfully predicted that Akbar
would at last have sons, lived on the hill as a
recluse. Fatehpur Sikri was Akbar's capital
for just fourteen years, and remained a ghost
city thereafter. Seen through the colonnade
is one of the most famous of its buildings, the
Diwan-i-Khass or Hall of Private Audience.

above Looking through the House of Raja Birbal at Fatehpur Sikri.
The carving is exceptionally profuse, evoking Gujarati woodcarving
(p. 67), suggesting that craftsmen were imported from that recently
conquered region. The styles of both architecture and decoration
are a Hindu contribution to the Mughal capital.

opposite, above, and above A festoon of tassels hangs in a long border
on one of the red sandstone buildings at Fatehpur Sikri.
Such tassels formed part of the trappings of elephants and horses
on ceremonial occasions (cf. p. 97). Below is a border of
chevrons, greatly favoured by the Mughals.

Vertical borders with flowers, fruits and leaves on undulating stems
are an ornament on many of the red sandstone buildings
of Fatehpur Sikri.

above left The flowers alternately placed on scrolling stems here
may be based on the honeysuckle, a delicious reminder for the Mughal
emperor and his court of their summer retreat in Kashmir.

opposite, and above right On the Pavilion of the Turkish Sultana, which
has some of the finest stone carving, perhaps created by Gujarati
craftsmen, pomegranates on the main stem alternate with grapes on
the ends of graceful sideshoots. (For the ornament of the Pavilion,
see also pp. 149 and 196–97.)

above Detail of a façade in the Jahangiri Mahal in the
Red Fort at Agra, built by Akbar in the 1560s–70s. Geometric panels
are accompanied by borders based on plant forms at the top of the wall
and around the niche on the right.

opposite, above, and above In the Red Fort at Agra highly stylized
flowers are framed within the abstract 'lotus in profile' motif and
accompanied by leaves, the pattern alternately inverted along the
length of the border carved in red sandstone.

above, and opposite, above The plinth of Shah Jahan's Diwan-i Amm or
Hall of Public Audience in the Red Fort at Agra, completed in 1637, is
ornamented with three horizontal borders, the upper two more deeply
carved than the lowest one. For the central motif, the designer
devised repeated cartouches with an iris-like flower.

above The Red Fort covers a vast area, with buildings of different
dates in different states of preservation, the majority in varying shades
of red sandstone.

A white marble parapet in the Red Fort at Agra is composed of
iris motifs set in cartouches separated by cypress trees. A most elegant
and refined piece of work, it demonstrates the perfection that
the Emperor Shah Jahan's masons were capable of achieving
in their work for him between 1628 and 1637.

above, and opposite, above A motif of a figleaf enclosing three figs is repeated in a band of beautifully carved marble, characteristic of the work in the Red Fort at Agra under Shah Jahan, when many of the red sandstone buildings were replaced with white marble.

above The inner chamber of the Mussaman Burj, a palatial interior
created for Shah Jahan in the Red Fort. Rich *pietra dura* borders
surround the deep niches with delicately cusped arches, used to hold
lamps and scent bottles, and the dado with its exquisitely carved floral
motifs. *Pietra dura* also ornaments the marble pool.

The town of Jaisalmer in Rajasthan, seen from the top of one of the very grand merchants' *havelis*. On the skyline is the magnificent fort, its outer wall studded with serried ranks of circular bastions. At its highest point, centre left, is the old palace, the Juna Mahal. The local honey-yellow sandstone is soft and easy to carve when freshly quarried, then hardens after long exposure to the elements.

Jaisalmer has few rivals in India for rich surface decoration on architecture – a reflection of just how wealthy the town had grown on the vital trade routes where it lay as a caravanserai in the Thar Desert. Seen here is a detail of the late 19th-century Mandir Palace, which lies outside the fort, down in the town.

At the centre is a shallow ornamental *jharoka* or covered balcony filled with a *jali*, its roof forming an accentuated semicircle and its base an inverted pyramid made up from a fan of leaves. The ornamentation of the whole wall is predominantly composed of symmetrical panels and borders, almost all based on plant motifs. The two panels that flank the *jharoka* (see also *opposite*) incorporate peacocks. The inclusion of the peacock is significant: while it represents India as a whole, it is really the royal bird of Rajasthan. At the far left is a small shrine with a figure of a god.

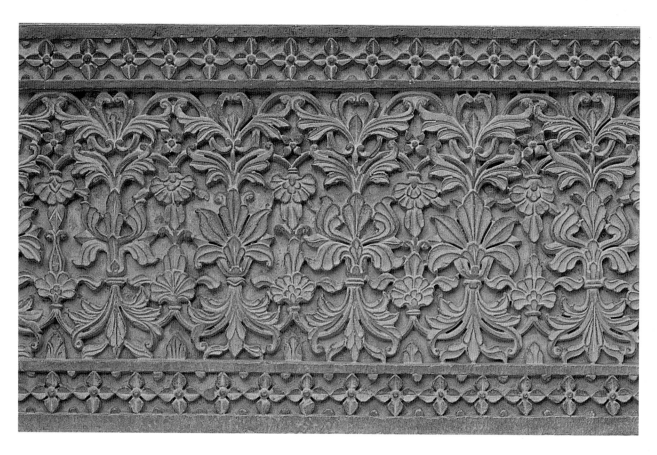

The ornament in this band in the Mandir Palace complex at
Jaisalmer bears no resemblance to any known botanical species,
yet it is inimitably and exuberantly floral. The pattern can be read
as repeating columns of flamboyant symmetrically carved foliage,
united along the top by a broken undulating line. The 'columns'
are additionally linked by pendant stylized flowers near the top and
inverted flower crowns at the bottom. Narrow borders of simple four-
petalled flowers frame the main design; at the bottom, shown in the
drawing, is a more ornate border of foliage linked by curved 'stems'
with decorative loops.

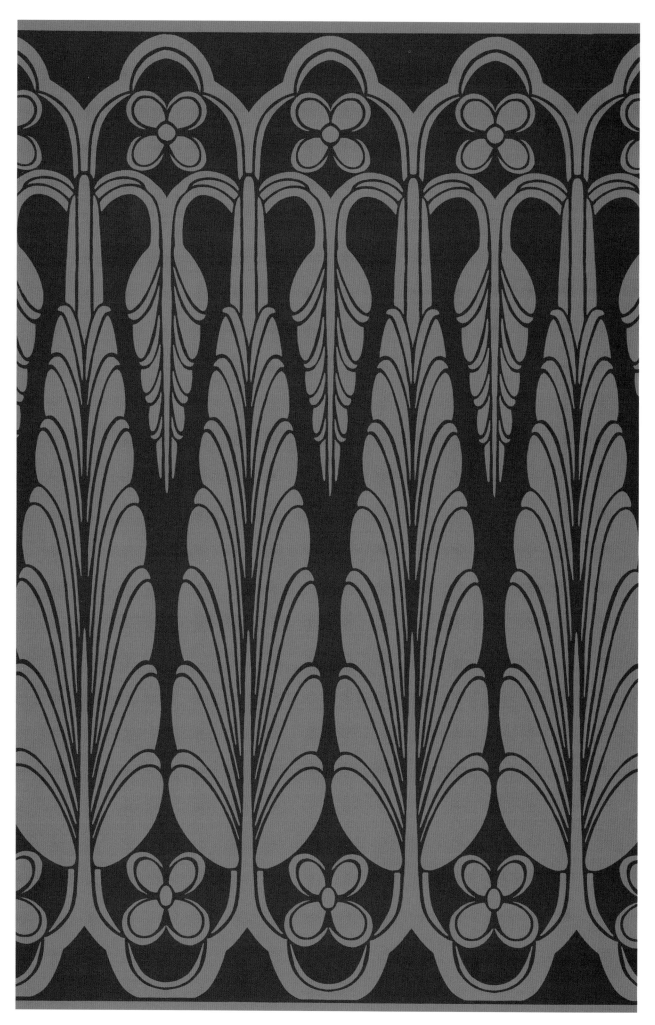

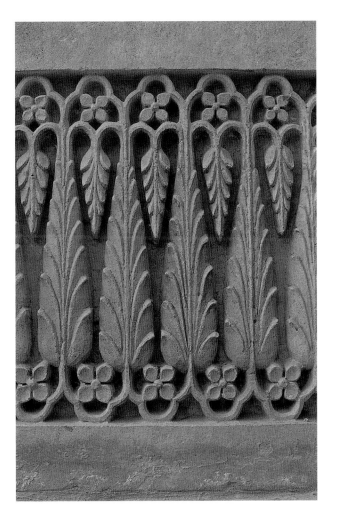

opposite, and above left This carved decoration in the Mandir Palace complex at Jaisalmer is based on the Persian motif of the cypress tree, both upright and, in a smaller form, inverted. Four-petalled flowers fill the voids at the top and bottom in a restrained manner, in keeping with the rest of the design.

above right Looking through a cusped arch to the Jawahar Vilas, with its pediment displaying a coat of arms – a touch of European influence. The building is raised on a high plinth, and the cantilevered staircases have balustrades carved with stylized leaves. Nothing could be more traditional than the very fine *jharoka* at the centre, a showpiece of the finest stonemason's work with its extraordinarily rich detail, curved *bangla* eaves, and delicately sculpted dome. The rich façade is articulated by vertical and horizontal bands.

Maheshwar in Madhya Pradesh, on the bank of the sacred
Narmada River, is an important place of pilgrimage. It was the
capital of the great warrior Queen Ahilya Bai Holkar, regarded as
a holy figure, and the Shaivite Ahilyeshwar Temple was built and
dedicated to her by her successor, Yeshwant Rao I, in 1805–12. Almost
every part of the complex is carved with floral motifs, seen particularly
richly in the highly decorated arcade along the temple front; in the
centre is a small *jharoka* with voluptuous *bangla* eaves and dome. (For the
decoration of the temple, see the following pages and pp. 166–67.)

The piers of the arcade at the Ahilyeshwar Temple at Maheshwar
(see p. 93) are carved with vertical bands in which squares and
rectangles are repeated one above the other. Flanking the carvings are
strips of deeply incised eight-pointed stars, and beyond them
on either side a rope and stylized leaves.

above left, and opposite The squares are filled with a single
multi-petalled flower set in a star from whose eight points sprout
fleur-de-lis-like leaves; the inner line of the star can be read as a
stylized lotus. The rectangles hold a chain-linked cartouche filled
with a bold daisy-like flower and lush foliage.

above right The bases of the piers have the ancient motif of the
vase of plenty, with sprays of leaves and flowers on long stems
not unlike irises.

above, and opposite, above In this border on the Ahilyeshwar Temple
at Maheshwar (see pp. 92–93) cusped arches frame peacocks and,
inverted, frame flowers. This cusped shape – perhaps a stylized profile
of the lotus in bloom – appears right across central and north-west
India on Hindu and Mughal monuments alike.

opposite, below Along the entire length of the plinth of a smaller temple
in the complex is a playfully animated cavalcade of elephants.
They wear their full festive regalia, including necklace-like garlands.
The head of the elephant in the centre is carved in the round and
looks directly out. Some see the elephant motif as
symbolizing monsoon clouds.

Detail of a carved stone design on the wall of a roof terrace of the Juna Mahal that looks over the valley in which the town of Dungarpur is nestled. From the symbolic cypress tree a stylized floral motif explodes, with acanthus leaves, a chrysanthemum-like flower at the centre, and various leaf shapes which form a cusped semicircle. The overall design is enhanced by its arresting symmetry. The main motif is flanked by a very similar but smaller half-repeat.

The Udai Bilas Palace at Dungarpur was built by Udai Singh II
in the mid-19th century. This arch over a doorway in the main inner
courtyard, carved in the local greenish-grey sandstone, is bordered
by an elongated semicircle of interlocking cusps and a row of acanthus
leaves. In the spandrels are deep-cut compositions of peacocks,
flowers and leaves. The rich border above has a pair of peacocks
searching for food in the vigorous foliage (see the detail in
the drawing *opposite*). Between them is a motif with an elaborate flower
in a frame, flanked by a similar motif split down the middle
and laid on its side. This framed flower motif alternates
with a framed cypress tree.

above left The Quwwat ul-Islam ('Might of Islam') Mosque,
with the great tower known as the Qutb Minar, was begun in 1193 by
the Muslim Qutb-ud-din Aibak to mark his victory over Hindu Delhi,
re-using some material from Hindu and Jain temples and using
Hindu craftsmen for the new work. In the foreground is the Alai
Darwaza, a gate added in the early 14th century, which is a masterful
display of the red sandstone and white marble that were to become
such a favoured combination in the Mughal period.

above right, and opposite The monumental screen or 'Great Arch' of
the mosque, built in 1199, includes wonderfully conceived and carved
vertical bands which could be read as foliage or as a vigorous stream
of water frothing with bubbles and foam – either way, an explosive
exposition of the kinetic energy of nature (see also pp. 104–5).

above left The early 13th-century tomb of Sultan Iltutmish forms part
of the Qutb Minar complex south of Delhi. His cenotaph, itself
with a band of decoration, is surrounded by walls – here we see the
mihrab – covered with the most intricately carved bands of Quranic
inscriptions in various scripts. None of the material here was re-used
from temples on the site.

above right, and opposite A detail from the monumental screen of the
Quwwat ul-Islam Mosque, carved by Hindu craftsmen in 1199. Next
to the left-hand border with its explosion of energy (see pp. 102–3) is
a vigorous exposition of the lotus. The multiplied thick stems have a
muscular assertiveness; slimmer spiralling stems end with the
lotus in its various stages.

Fat lotus blossoms spring from a sturdy undulating stem on one of the four wonderful *toranas* or gates to the Great Stupa at Sanchi, a Buddhist holy place dating from the 1st century BC–1st century AD (see p. 162). Considering the age of these masterpieces it is extraordinary that they have survived the elements so long. The lotus flowers crammed into a confined space promise bounty and have attracted birds.

The Shiv Niwas in the City Palace at Udaipur was begun by Maharana
Sajjan Shambhu Singh in 1874 and finished at the beginning of the
20th century. Part of it remains the private home of the Maharana of
Udaipur. The anteroom seen here looks out over Lake Pichola, with
the Aravali Hills in the distance. Multiple bands of decoration are
created in finely cut painted glass (see pp. 110–11). Ceiling and walls
are framed in a running scroll with a stylized flower at the centre
(detail *opposite*), and the spandrel of the arch has a dramatic scroll.

A detail of the cornice and the ceiling border in an anteroom in the Shiv Niwas in the City Palace at Udaipur (see p. 108). Although a comparatively late work, it follows the Rajput tradition of using colour to make a decorative statement. Glass is a notoriously difficult material to cut and shape, and the craftsmen here achieved the highest standard of finish.

The painted glass and mirror-glass work in the mid-19th-century
Udai Bilas Palace at Dungarpur is some of the finest in Rajasthan.
In this vertical scrolling design in a bedroom the work has a naivety
which, combined with the luminosity and sheen of the glass, lends the
motif a lively fluidity. In each unit a lotus bloom is set at the heart
of a sensuous scroll of foliage and lotus buds.

opposite A vertical motif in the main courtyard of the Udai Bilas Palace at Dungarpur, where it is carved in the local stone. The bold undulating stem is decorated with the lotus in its various stages – in bud form, as a fully opened flower, and with seedpods.

right One of the walls in a bedroom, with decoration created in painted glass and mirror glass set in plaster (cf. p. 113). Completed in a realistic botanical fashion, this too shows the lotus in its various stages of growth. The plant springs out of a symbolic vase, which has a pair of birds sitting on its shoulders. The plaster background is powdered with mirror-glass leaves and with fish, insects, and even a turtle.

At the heart of the City Palace at Jaipur in Rajasthan is the Sri Niwas, a suite of mirrored rooms (see pp. 38–41).

opposite, above, and above In one of the rooms, a narrow border with a repeating pattern of ornate gesso against a background of chips of mirror glass runs along the cornice. The artist framed his design in a cartouche made up of right angles, loops and pointed arches and filled the space with flowers seen frontally and in profile, with additional buds and foliage.

opposite, below In this small room the walls from the dado upwards are covered in chips of mirror glass in an arresting composition of rectangular shapes. The ceiling is also entirely set with mirror glass in a bold floral pattern, above a row of profile portraits (see p. 39).

A detail of the multiple bands of ornament at the top of the walls of the central room of the Sri Niwas in the City Palace of Jaipur (see p. 38). Variously shaped cartouches filled with symmetrical floral motifs backed with mirror glass are separated by thin bands of single flowers with leaves. Repetition and symmetry are important ingredients in the overall design.

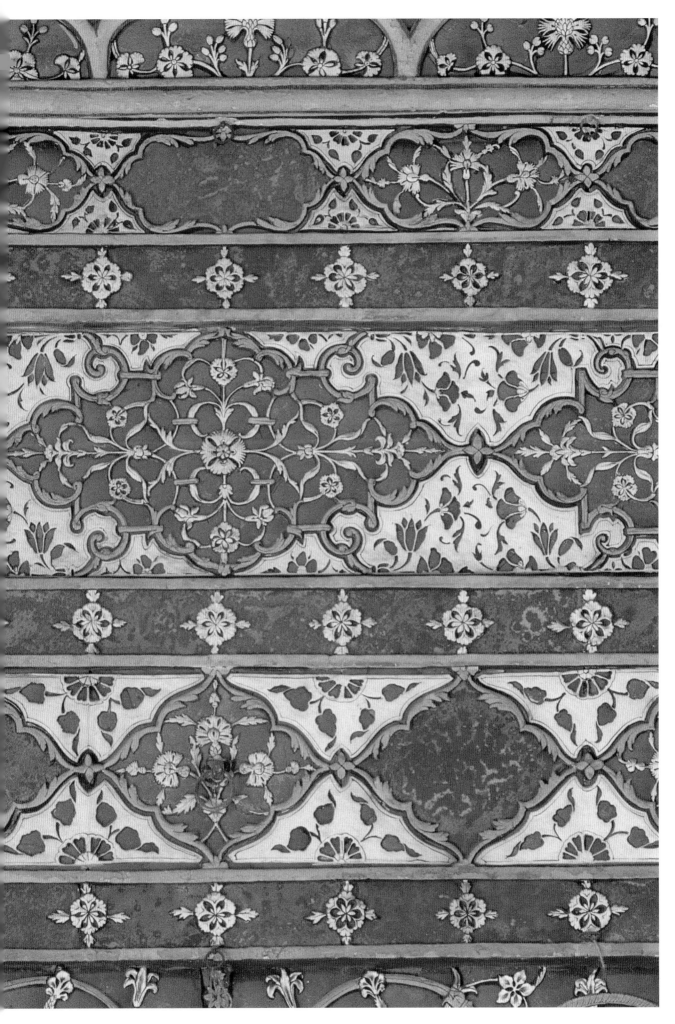

above, and opposite, above The ceiling ornament in the Diwan-i-Amm
or Hall of Public Audience in the City Palace at Jaipur is created
in plaster and paint. The broad open design is filled with sprays of
flowers; a scroll effect is used in the lower part of the composition, and
in alternating elements a spray of flowers springs from a stylized vase.
The Diwan-i-Amm is a colonnaded hall open on four sides. Giant
silver vessels here held Ganges water for royal rituals.

opposite, below The dramatic vault over one of the doorways in the
Pritam Niwas Chowk in the City Palace. The bodies of the peacocks
are three-dimensional, set against recesses where their tails are
painted. The spaces between the recesses are filled with a chevron
pattern, as is the area above the cusped arch. In the centre is
a figure of a Hindu god.

Detail of a dado in the Juna Mahal at Dungarpur, painted in a light tone on a dramatic black background. The central band is framed by narrow borders of flower and leaf motifs. In the main design, an undulating line links two alternating motifs: in one, shown in the drawing, a single large flower is placed in the middle, while in the other, seen in the photograph, leaves curl outward and multiple shoots spring almost symmetrically upward and down.

The Samode Haveli is the Jaipur home of the rawals of Samode, whose palace lies at the head of a ravine just inside the boundary of the Aravali Hills. This 19th-century wall-painting in the dining area (the palace is now a luxury hotel) recalls the garden of their palace: an energetic rose with blossoms and buds sends its scrolling stems round and through a repeating set of circles, linked by a rose. Generously scattered throughout the border are birds, butterflies and insects.

Opening off at either end of the dining area of the Samode Haveli
are two small rooms with rich painted decoration in blue and white,
the colours of Jaipur pottery, for which the city has long been famed.

opposite, above left and below left In one room the dado is painted with
trees and birds, reminders of the garden. The walls and ceiling have
a lattice pattern; on the ceiling flowers soften the intersections of the
grid, while on the walls the lattice is overlaid by a delicate scrolling
pattern with stylized irises at the centre of alternate rows of diamonds.
The concave cornice has a pattern of intertwining stems that is
repeated, with slight variations, elsewhere in these rooms.

opposite, above right The concave cornice of the other little room, which
also has intersecting ovals from which emerge delicately sinuous
stems with leaves. The main flowers are life-like morning glory.

opposite, below right Multiple bands decorate a ceiling.

above Drawing of part of a morning glory pattern on the cornice of
one of the rooms (cf. *opposite, above left and right*).

opposite An arch in the upper wall of the double-height Durbar Hall
of Samode Palace (see p. 182). The rich polychrome decoration is
dense and exquisitely finished. It was created by local artists; their
descendants still practise their art in the little village of Samode, and
are called in when any repair is needed. The motifs are predominantly
floral, but include figures such as those who would have inhabited
the room when it was created in the 19th century. The main wall of
the room beyond, at first-floor level, is painted in a single colour on a
white background (see p. 232), creating a dramatic counterpoint.

above An analytical drawing of the acanthus leaf border used in the
Durbar Hall at cornice level and, inverted, below the upper stage.

The Bundi Palace in Rajasthan, dating from the mid-18th century, is one of the older Rajput palaces. It is famous for its wall-paintings, but it is off the beaten track and rapidly falling into disrepair: many areas are now said to be dangerous to visit.

above The cloister-like Chitra Shali has some of the finest paintings in any of the early palaces. Fighting elephants, stylized flowers in vases and paintings of palace life are framed in varied borders.

opposite Detail of the design of the dado in an apartment in the palace, where this vase and flowers motif is repeated horizontally. The original is finished in gold leaf. The vase is supported on a stand and flanked by two small jars. Looped sawtooth-edged cusps surround the composition, which is framed above and below by narrow borders.

3

Single Motifs
& Panels

Motifs set out as single features by their nature attract attention. They decorate architectural elements such as the bases and tops of pillars (e.g. pp. 144–45, 148–49) and provide focal points for walls and ceilings (e.g. pp. 174–77). They may also be used as features on the top of a wall (pp. 158–59). They can be more than purely decorative. They can be a pictorial language, and, in certain cases, a subtle form of political propaganda; and they can demonstrate the migration of features, in such elements as the cypress tree and the long-necked vase.

They include religious motifs. On the Chaumukha Jain temple at Ranakpur there is an exceptional piece of marble carving with a Hindu divinity at its heart surrounded by *apsaras*, heavenly nymphs whose tails join intricately woven lotus stems (pp. 164–65). And another *apsara* appears as the central figure in an ornament on the carved wood façade of a merchant's *haveli* in Ahmedabad, dancing and holding billowing vegetation (pp. 190–91).

The vase of flowers is one of the most ubiquitous images in the subcontinent's repertoire of floral motifs. Symbolizing abundance, it is equally significant for Hindus, Jains, Buddhists and Muslims, and appears in a gamut of guises. It features in particularly varied form on the walls of the Jai Mandir in the Amber Fort, where the flowers in some cases share the vase with various types of fruit (pp. 154–57).

Two other single motifs that go beyond the purely decorative are Islamic in origin and were imported from Persia by the Mughals. The cypress tree, seen on the tomb of Itimad-ud-Daula in Agra (pp. 198–99), was adopted by Hindu patrons; on a column of the portico of the Udai Bilas Palace at Dungarpur in Rajasthan its form has been changed, and its upright tip curves over (p. 160). The long-necked vase often appears on buildings, for instance in the compound of the tomb of the Emperor Akbar at Sikandra (pp. 134–37). A number of the vases at Akbar's tomb have flowers in them, and additionally the craftsmen have included specifically Indian creatures, elephants and peacocks – a fine demonstration of the Mughal ethos of inclusivity.

A pair of peacocks are marvellously rendered on a horizontal bar of one of the *toranas*, the magnificent stone gateways of the ancient Buddhist site of Sanchi (pp. 162–63). The peacock from early times has been a symbol of regal authority, and the image shows that our perception of beauty has remained little changed over two millennia.

Not far from Sanchi is the now deserted city of Mandu. Here in the arch of a blind opening on a building constructed for pre-Mughal Muslim patrons the bulk of the space is filled with a stylized lotus – a quintessentially Indian motif – in full bloom (pp. 172–73).

✳✳

The decoration of the eastern gate of the enclosure surrounding the tomb of the Mughal Emperor Akbar at Sikandra near Agra, completed in 1613, includes arch-topped panels filled with geometrical ornament in coloured stone and a narrow vertical strip of red sandstone panels carved with long-necked vases (cf. p. 137)

above, and opposite Long-necked vases carved in red sandstone,
set in arches, in the precinct of Akbar's tomb at Sikandra. One is more
elaborate, with three peacocks at the top. In the spandrels are rosettes;
lining the inner edges of the arches are linked honey- or water-pots,
held aloft by pairs of elephants. The vases are a motif imported from
Persia, whereas the elephants and pots are Hindu elements.

overleaf Details of the recessed arch in the western gate to the
tomb. Most of the surfaces are painted with fictive arched niches and
cusped horizontal cartouches. In the centre near the top floral motifs
take over, and the main arch is filled with a giant-leafed plant
springing from a vase.

This composition of single motifs on the exterior of the tomb of Itimad-ud-Daula at Agra, completed in 1628 (see pp. 28–33), is an elegiac reflection of the elegant good life that was enjoyed at the court of the Mughal Emperor Jahangir, Itimad-ud-Daula's father-in-law: vases filled with narcissus, ornamented long-necked vases with serpent-like handles, and decorated tumblers are set in cusped niches as they would have been in reality, but all realized in *pietra dura*, coloured stone inlaid in white marble.

The riverfront courtyard of the Jahangiri Mahal in the Red Fort at Agra, built in the 1560s–70s, is overlooked by façades articulated in the classic Mughal fashion (see also pp. 34–35). Here the blind arches in the red sandstone are outlined with white marble. The uppermost section, divided up into panels filled with carving, is a false wall, creating a private space on the roof open to the air. At the right is a kiosk with angled eaves and a *chhatri* at the top. A narrow water channel circumscribes the courtyard, and a fountain would have danced in the centre. Just visible at the far left is part of one of the columns of the verandah (see p. 145).

opposite above left A view of the riverfront flank of the
Red Fort at Agra. The raised terrace supports the courtyard of the
Jahangiri Mahal (see pp. 34–35). In the foreground is a beautifully
carved *jali*, and the low balustrade is treated like a stone screen.

opposite below left and above right The columns in the double-height
verandah are decorated with chevrons, and their bases have a sensuous
flow of curves alluding to leaves and flowers (*above*).

opposite below right A contrasting note is struck by this panel seen in
raking light. The pattern is of particular interest since it includes one
of the most potent Hindu symbols, the swastika.

The Emperor Shah Jahan, whose love of marble conformed to his luxurious tastes, when he came to the throne in 1628 quickly set about creating his own architectural legacy within the forts at both Agra and Delhi, and the majority of the new buildings were completed in marble. White in the Islamic tradition is consistent with the ideals of purity, goodness and spirituality. In this room in the Musamman Burj area of the Agra Fort the walls are faced with simple panels and with more elaborate designs of arches made up of stylized leaves and flowers. The rich effect is increased by the use of gilding.

A capital on the verandah of the Pavilion of the Turkish Sultana at Fatehpur Sikri, the new city begun by the Emperor Akbar in 1571. (While it is known as the 'Pavilion of the Turkish Sultana', this was probably a *mardana* pavilion, used to house men of the palace.) Within the scalloped outer edges are stylized floral motifs. The stone is cut like a perfect block for hand-printing textiles, leaving ridges to carry the dye (cf. pp. 9, 10).

The Amber Fort was begun by the Rajput ruler Man Singh (r. 1592–1615) and subsequently added to. With a good monsoon season the artificial lake below it fills, helping to change the whole ambience of the valley. In winter a wispy fog rises from the surface of the water as the early morning sun progressively lights the fort's magnificent frontage. Ernest Havell, a British arts administrator in India in the years around 1900, wrote of Rajput palaces: 'If our poets had sung them, our painters pictured them, our heroes and famous men lived in them, their romantic beauty would be on every man's lips in Europe.'

The Jai Mandir in the Raj Mahal in the Amber Fort was built by Mirza Jai Singh (r. 1623–68) and functioned as his private apartment. It is surrounded on three sides by an arcaded verandah. Its upper surfaces both outside and in are incrusted with mirrorwork, while its white marble dados are carved with floral motifs, both in single panels and grouped in tiered compositions, in *pietra dura* frames. The floral theme strongly recalls examples in the Mughal Red Fort at Agra (cf. p. 83). The Hindu patron may have been to Agra and been inspired, or it may be that craftsmen who had worked at Agra came here in search of work. Some of the floral compositions recall compositions that Mughal artists derived from European herbals (*above and opposite*), while others are more elaborate and incorporate vases (*following pages*). A beautifully rendered butterfly or moth adds to the realism.

Vases richly filled with flowers – a motif imported from Persia, of symbolic importance in both Muslim and Hindu India – are displayed both singly and in two tiers on the marble dados of the Jai Mandir in the Raj Mahal in the Amber Fort complex (see p. 152). Occasionally a vase also carries fruit, as here, where we can clearly identify a fig and pomegranates that have split, exposing their seeds.

overleaf Drawing of part of a dado, with vases of flowers superimposed in two tiers. The vases themselves have an extraordinary variety of decoration, and many types of flowers are shown, including lotus and dahlias. Frozen in marble, they retain an extraordinary freshness and animation.

preceding pages Life-size peacocks on exuberant scrolls of foliage flank stone gatepiers within the complex of the Udai Bilas Palace at Dungarpur, begun in the mid-19th century. Steps descend to the lake; beyond is the island temple, the royal household's private place of worship.

opposite Drawing of a cypress tree carved in relief on a column of the portico at the entrance to the Udai Bilas Palace. In this design the tree curves over at the top, a motif that some have interpreted as reflecting the adaptation of this Persian motif to India; others have seen in it the origin of the Paisley pattern.

right The Ek Thambia Mahal at the centre of the main courtyard of the palace rises out of a space originally filled with water. It is richly decorated with carved stone (including four large statues at the corners of the upper marble stage), sculpted plaster and pictorial mirror-glass mosaic. Note the balconies with curved roofs on the first overhanging stage, the white *chhatris* above them, and the *bangla* roof on the *chhatri* at the top.

The four sculpted *toranas* or gates of the Buddhist Great
Stupa at Sanchi, created in the 1st century BC–1st century AD, are by
some considered to be the greatest masterpieces of Indian art.
Captain Fell accidentally came across the ruins of Sanchi in 1819
and found himself unable to convey 'even a very faint idea of the
magnificence of such stupendous structures and exquisitely finished
sculpture'. The themes are both religious and secular. A wonderful
depiction of the lotus plant in flower climbs up one of the
gateposts (see pp. 106–7). In this scene a pair of feeding peacocks
are combined with two types of fruiting plant.

The monumental Jain temple at Ranakpur, in an isolated valley in
Rajasthan, was built in the mid-15th century by wealthy merchants.
It is dedicated to Adinath, one of the twenty-four Jain *Tirthankaras* or
pathfinders, and known as the Chaumukha Temple because it is four-
faced. It is famous for its double-height multi-faceted pillars.

above, and opposite above right An exquisite mandala-like sculpture with
a divinity in the centre, surrounded by *apsaras* – celestial nymphs –
whose tails tie in to knotted stems that sprout lotus buds and frame
open lotus blooms. In Indian mythology, whether Jain, Buddhist
or Hindu, the lotus can be a symbol of the unfolding universe,
emerging from water on the earth.

Self-contained motifs carved in stone on the Ahilyeshwar Temple
at Maheshwar, from the beginning of the 19th century (see pp. 92–97).

opposite above left, and above An elegant dome-like figure made up of
acanthus-like foliage, on the outer wall towards the Narmada River.
Peacocks flank the base, and parakeets perch half-way up.

opposite above right and below left Decoration on the plinth includes a lotus
flower and a maze-like zigzag geometric pattern with flowers.

opposite below right A stylized tree set on a very complicated base, next to
the riverfront entrance to the complex, catches the evening sun.

Mandu is one of India's fabled deserted cities.
Set on a crest of the Vindhya range and
surrounded by lakes, what had been a Hindu
site belonged to the Muslim Delhi Sultanate
until the beginning of the 15th century, when
the governor, Dilawar Khan, proclaimed
himself Sultan of Malwa; he was succeeded by
his son, Hoshang Shah. The city, which had
become the capital, was renamed Shadiabad,
City of Joy. There were not enough craftsmen
available locally, so the patrons turned to
Delhi; architecture there at the time was
Afghan-influenced, and Mandu has some of
the finest and largest buildings in that style on
the subcontinent. Construction went on up to
the mid-16th century. There are at least forty
ruins on the site. Seen here is a tomb, built
next to one of the lakes.

above A geometric pattern with hexagons and paired diagonal lines in a square, part of the ornament of an archway at Mandu (p. 172).

opposite above left Rupmati's Pavilion, poised on the edge of a dramatic escarpment. Rupmati, a renowned Hindu singer, was the lover of the Muslim Baz Bahadur, the last independent ruler. When he was defeated by troops of the Mughal Emperor Akbar in 1561 he fled, and she committed suicide.

opposite above right and below right The Jahaz Mahal at Mandu is also known as the 'Ship Palace' because of its shape and its position between two lakes. It was probably built by Sultan Ghiyas-ud-Din in the later 15th century for the women of the court. On the roof are open pavilions and elegant kiosks and this sensuously decorative water channel.

opposite below left The plateau is peppered with summerhouses, palaces and pavilions that had pools, fountains, loggias, domes, and even subterranean areas in which to escape from the summer heat.

This 15th-century archway at Mandu combines geometric and
floral ornament. The lower part is filled, as though with door panels,
by four squares decorated with hexagons and diagonal lines
(see p. 170). Above them, a stylized lotus like a rose window is set
between small stylized lotuses – a Hindu and also Buddhist motif,
appropriate in this region which in earlier days was home
to practitioners of both religions.

The Meherangarh or Majestic Fort at Jodhpur, largest of
the Rajput kingdoms, looks down from a rocky outcrop on the
thriving town, where the houses are painted an auspicious blue,
colour of the Lord Krishna's skin. Work began under Rao Jodha in the
mid-15th century. The shrine at the fort's entrance seems diminutive
in front of its towering walls. The decoration, carried out over many
centuries, includes this mirror-set ceiling rose finished in painted
glass mosaic (*above, and opposite, above right*) and stained glass windows set
in stonework carved and highlighted by gilding (*opposite, below left*).

A mirror on the ceiling of one of the royal sleeping quarters in
the Meherangarh at Jodhpur, set in a combination of low-relief
plasterwork and mirror- and painted glass inlay. The border
has stylized four-petalled flowers. Within that, a ring of looping cusps
surrounds the inner frame of the mirror, all in plaster relief.
The mirror is particularly effective here, creating spots of dancing
light as the viewer moves round below, looking up. In the setting,
the lotus motif recurs in the cusped semicircle of leaves
at the bottom of the design.

opposite A complex painted composition in a small room in the
City Palace of Udaipur. The shallow cusped arch is modelled in
low relief plasterwork and given the appearance of greater depth by
shadow-like painting. In the centre a panel composed of a delicate
plaster moulding and mirrorwork frames an Udaipur School
miniature of a nobleman on horseback. Just above the dado rail is a
striking intricate motif composed of spiralling branch-like fronds.
Below, two elephants engage in combat.

above When doubled, the pattern above the dado becomes a classic
motif symmetrical on both its vertical and horizontal axes, in this case
with a European flavour.

While the City Palace of Udaipur is one of the older Rajput palaces, succeeding generations have put their own stamps on their architectural inheritance.

left The decorators took full advantage of the possibilities of painted glass mosaic, using it all over the palace rather than just in a *shish mahal*. The ornate motif of which half is shown here, over a niche in the staircase leading up to the royal apartments, is worked in raised plaster and coloured not with paint but with glass – a medium that remains bright and fresh.

opposite Drawing showing the complete design of similar decoration over another niche in the staircase.

opposite, and above left A medallion painted on the ceiling of the Diwan-i-
Amm, or Hall of Public Audience, in the City Palace of Jaipur.

above right Looking from the Diwan-i-Amm courtyard to the Ganesh
Pol, which leads to the private area of the palace and the Chandra
Mahal. Because of the climate in this region the walls are little
more than wonderful fretwork *jalis*, to allow free movement of air.
The building is topped by a *bangla* roof and domes. At Jaipur, as in a
Mughal complex, the residential buildings are independent of the
fortifications. The shallowness of the cusping of the arch is another
indication of a move away from pure Rajput architecture.

The magnificent double-height Durbar Hall of Samode Palace is entirely painted with floral motifs (for a detail, see p. 128).
On the ceiling (*above left*) they are held within a strong geometric network. Taken out of context, this might be a detail of a fine Indian rug. The Durbar Hall is still used today, since Samode Palace has been converted into one of the region's most successful heritage hotels.

opposite A motif taken from the broad band just above the arches.

right Looking through an arch from the
dining area to a small space in the Samode
Haveli in Jaipur, the town palace of the
rawals. The painter has exploited the effects
both of reversing the two tones and of varying
the scale of the motifs. Around the arch
colour serves as the background and the
floral motifs are in white, in negative; in the
space beyond, the painting is dark – positive –
against a pale background. The motifs round
the arch are much smaller in scale and the
surface is densely covered, whereas on the
wall beyond the trees at dado level have a light
airiness. The floral design on the upper part
of the wall makes the strongest statement in
the overall composition.

opposite The beautifully executed
symmetrical floral design incorporates iris
in full flower and in bud. The outer sprays
undulate upwards, curving in at the top;
the seemingly erratic character of the leaves
gives the design an innate energy, while the
vertical, fully open iris in the centre holds the
eye with confidence.

above left The magnificent fortified palace of Junagarh
looks out at the back over gardens, a hugely impressive achievement in
the desert setting of Bikaner in Rajasthan (see p. 64). The pyramid-
topped pavilion faced with blue tiles is the Chhatra Mahal, formerly
used as an airy bedchamber in the burning heat of summer.

above right All the surfaces in the Anup Mahal are breathtakingly
decorated with floral motifs in gilded gesso against *sang-de-boeuf* red
(see also pp. 250–53). In the spacious alcove with a *bangla* roof, set with
velvet cushions and bolsters, the maharaja throned at meetings.

opposite An analytical drawing of the dense voluptuous foliage
immediately above the capital of the fluted column. At the heart of the
design is a poppy with its distinctive seedpod.

Detail of the carved teakwood façade of a merchant's
haveli in the old quarter of Ahmedabad in Gujarat. The entablature,
with its elaborate sequence of horizontal bands, includes an ornament
with a dancing *apsara*, or celestial nymph, indicating that this is a
Hindu household. The theatrically unfurling foliage ending in
scrolls that the *apsara* holds, with shoots spiralling off to left and right,
increases the sense of animation.

4

Ornamental
Scenes

Ornamental scenes reflect the coalescence of years of practice and accumulated experience, ingenuity, countless flights of fancy, and a collaboration between craftsman and patron. They encompass a broad range of subject-matter, with, however, the natural world remaining the focus of interest. Delight in botanical forms underlies the scenes found on Muslim buildings. At the Taj Mahal, in the traditionally symbolic vase of flowers an iris and iris buds are surrounded by a halo of narcissus (p. 195), while on the Pavilion of the Turkish Sultana at Fatehpur Sikri a forestscape, perfect for the scene of a royal hunt, is depicted with such refinement that it resembles a Persian miniature (pp. 196–97). On the marble exterior of the tomb of Itimad-ud-Daula at Agra a large cypress tree and two smaller ones, elements both natural and symbolic, are surrounded by swirling creepers (pp. 198–99). More vigorously scrolling forms sprouting from one tree envelop another on an exceptional stone *jali* in the diminutive Sidi Sayed Mosque in Ahmedabad (pp. 209–11).

The carved stonework at Jaisalmer is altogether more fanciful and unrestrained (pp. 200–207). The rich floral imagery has an element of unreality here in the heart of the Thar Desert, and shows just how powerful the dream was of an idealized garden. It must have been astonishing to arrive in Jaisalmer with a camel caravan from the desert.

The monumental City Palace complex on the bank of Lake Pichola at Udaipur (pp. 212–13) hardly needed further embellishment. However, the craftsmen excelled with delicate work in glass, the most awkward of materials to manipulate, and dados in the Shiv Niwas are decorated with scenes of cranes feeding on the lakeside (pp. 214–15). Artists working with the same material filled the walls of the Shish Mahal in the Juna Mahal at Dungarpur with remarkable large mirror-glass mosaics of flowering trees and shrubs (pp. 218, 223).

In other parts of the City Palace in Udaipur painters covered the walls with displays of nature's bounty – flowering shrubs alive with birds (p. 241). In the Chavi Niwas in the City Palace at Jaipur the painting on plaster has an altogether looser and more animated feel to it. The walls are finished in a refreshing blue and white, enlivened with loops and energetic spirals of flourishing vegetation as well as varied flowering shrubs (pp. 242–45).

The decoration of the Anup Mahal in the Junagarh Fort in Bikaner is a Rajput masterclass in regal pomp (pp. 248–51). The dark red walls are brought to life with delicate gilded gesso work: in this, one of the most exotic of rooms, the floral motif is presented in its most sophisticated avatar.

opposite, and above The Taj Mahal at Agra is the tomb of Mumtaz
Mahal, favourite wife of the Mughal Emperor Shah Jahan, who died
in 1631. Built of white marble to represent the house of the Queen in
Paradise, it was completed in 1643. Its exquisite low-relief marble
carving includes this scene inside the tomb, where a variety of flowers
in a vase, with an upstanding central iris, are accompanied by two
plants growing symmetrically out of the ground.

overleaf A composition of trees and flowers in the dado of the Pavilion
of the Turkish Sultana at Fatehpur Sikri, the red sandstone city begun
by the Emperor Akbar in 1571 (see also pp. 75, 149).

Detail of an exterior wall of the tomb of Itimad-ud-Daula at Agra, completed in 1628 (see pp. 28–33), with two scenes in *pietra dura*. The smaller scene has a welcoming composition of a tray holding a covered cup, pomegranates and grapes, set in a curvaceous cartouche. The larger scene is rich with symbolism. The upstanding cypress trees are regarded by Sufi mystics as an embodiment of divine glory, and for poets they represent the beloved. The creepers with the lightness of touch of a dancer spiral up and around them, their leaves resembling those of the maple trees in the Mughals' beloved Kashmir Valley. The scene is a delicate visual interpretation of the Tree of Life of ancient Mesopotamian origin, promising immortality.

The late 19th-century Mandir Palace at Jaisalmer in Rajasthan,
dominated by an ornamental pavilion of characteristic Rajput shape,
is rich with carved and painted ornament.

above, and opposite, above right A pair of peahens flank a symbolic flower-
filled vase of plenty, the whole framed by a floral arch.

opposite, below left Detail of a courtyard wall (see p. 203) with a richly
carved *jharoka*. The palace priest has painted an auspicious swastika.

opposite, below right The inside of an arch, painted with a pair of
parakeets and flowering creepers.

above, and opposite, above Two peacocks are seen in this stone garden
carved on the Mandir Palace at Jaisalmer. Between them are what may
be banana leaves. Below, flowering plants are topped with smaller
birds, and the false window is framed by a flowering creeper
with small peacocks.

opposite, below A simple arch surrounded by highly intricate
carving leads from one courtyard to another. The plain walls are set
with ornamental *jharokas* and openings to light rooms behind.
The large *jharokas* are echoed by two miniature *jharokas* beside
the door (cf. p. 200).

The richness of the carving on the Mandir
Palace at Jaisalmer is extraordinary, and the
richness of the vegetation is paradoxical,
since unlike Mandu or Udaipur, which
have numerous lakes and sources of water,
Jaisalmer is in the middle of a desert.
Here a grapevine-like plant with energetic
scrolling forms is the dominant motif in
the centre. Above the carved demi-columns
left and right are large acanthus leaves.
The balcony has floral shapes in its openwork
trefoils, and from it hang two rows of
fruit- or cone-like pendants.

Rajput architecture lost momentum in the late 18th century,
but there was a brief revival in the 19th century before the taste for
European forms took over. The Mandir Palace at Jaisalmer (*above*) was
built long after the need for fortification had passed. One of the many
attractions of the Rajput style is its unpredictability, the constant
play of protruding and receding planes, and the plethora of
ornamental decorative elements.

opposite Motifs on a stone panel that leans up against a wall, discarded,
in a quiet corner of the palace. The outer panels left and right have
bold sprays of leaves with attendant parakeets; the two central panels,
in contrast, have plants that are small and detailed and a greater
variety of birds.

Gujarat was known for its wealth and superb textiles, and this is
reflected in the designs of the *jalis* with strongly contrasting patterns
that light the Sidi Sayed Mosque in Ahmedabad, built in 1573
in the time of the Muslim Sultanate.

above A strictly geometric composition of squares carved with a
dazzling variety of patterns.

above and overleaf One of two highly original *jalis* at the mosque:
a slender, straight palm tree stands at the centre of the composition,
while a bold curving tree winds up in front and explodes into a mass
of voluptuously delicate tendrils loaded with blossoms.
Such a creation required remarkable technical skill as well as artistic
inventiveness: a great many thin slabs of stone are individually
perforated with a small section of the pattern, and then delicately
pinned together to complete the overall design.

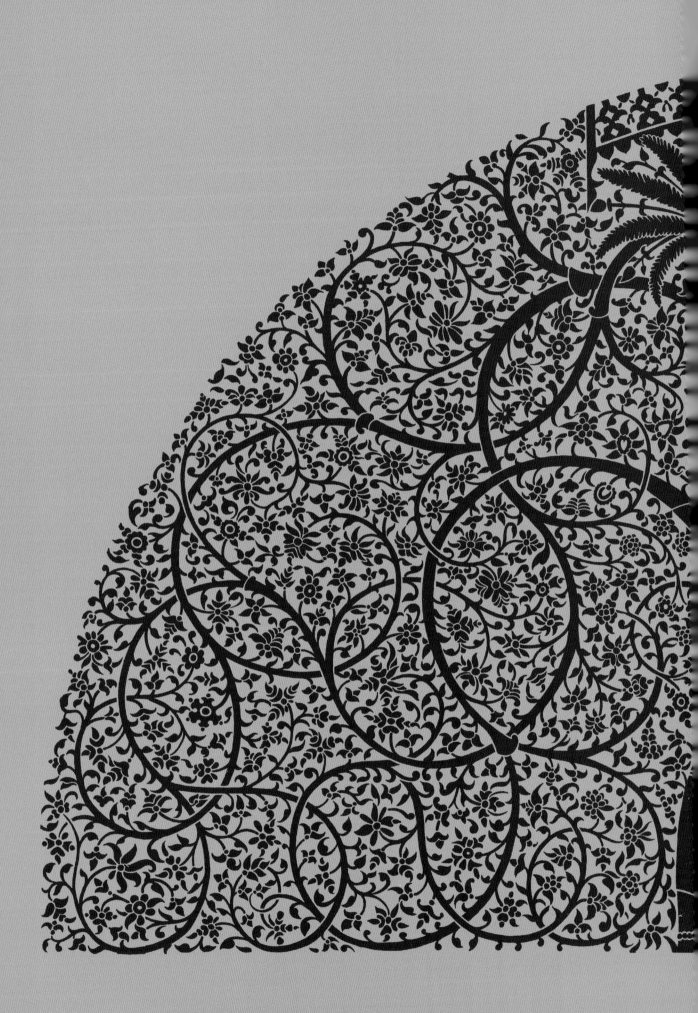

Looking across Lake Pichola at part of the
City Palace in Udaipur. From left to right,
the elements seen here are the Fateh Prakash,
named after Maharana Fateh Singh, who
ruled Mewar with his capital at Udaipur
from 1884 to 1930; the Shambu Nivas, private
apartments of the princely family; and the
Shiv Niwas, for royal guests. The forest to
the right is home to thousands of giant fruit
bats, which lumber out at dusk, skimming
the surface of the lake.

Details of dados in various rooms of the Shiv Niwas in the City
Palace of Udaipur. The birds in these compositions of coloured glass
and plaster are sarus and demoiselle cranes and guinea fowl. In the
monochrome design (*opposite, bottom*) the artist has inventively used
mirror glass for the water.

overleaf Drawing of one of the designs with cranes (*opposite, top*),
demonstrating its graphic power.

Every Rajput palace of any note has a *shish mahal*, a mirrored room
or pavilion, but each is unique in terms of its subject-matter or
theme. In the Juna Mahal at Dungarpur the emphasis is on flowering
trees and shrubs, wispy willow, and marigolds. The room becomes
particularly animated in the morning when the sun streaks through
the perforated openings along the left side of the room.

opposite Drawing of the composition to the left of the door. Energetic
sprays of foliage and giant marigolds are framed under a cusped arch.
At the bottom are peacocks seemingly in search of insects.

Drawings of mirror-glass mosaics in the dado of the
Shish Mahal in the Juna Mahal at Dungarpur (see p. 218). At the heart
of both compositions are flowering plants encircled by stylized leaves.
These are surrounded by broad borders filled with
dense floral motifs.

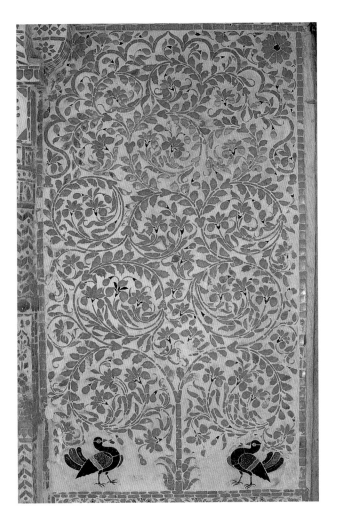

opposite, and above left For this flowering tree of mirror glass
in a wall panel in the Shish Mahal of the Juna Mahal at Dungarpur
(cf. p. 218) the artists chose dense scrolling forms, which have a
natural kinetic exuberance. Contrasting with the tree of mirror are
two birds in coloured glass.

above right In a small anteroom at one end of the Shish Mahal
the Maharaja and ladies of the court are depicted in mirror- and
coloured glass. The ruler, dressed in sumptuous clothing of which
the pattern is intricately reproduced, proffers a fully
open lotus flower.

above left A large ornamented vase flanked by banana plants forms a scene in the Juna Mahal at Dungarpur. In the dado rams charge a circular mirror (now missing). Silvery mirrorwork leaves gleam.

above right In this small room in the Aam Khass or private apartments everything is covered with mirror- or coloured glass. The ceiling has floral patterns and circular mirrors. The floor is of mirror, with designs painted in colour between the glass and its silvered backing. Scenes include the ruler receiving English visitors.

opposite Drawing of a glass mosaic in the room. Two birds face each other, while a third dives into the composition. Swirling vegetation grows out of a stylized pattern of piled-up mounds.

Peacocks and parakeets are positioned symmetrically beside
and above a circular mirror let into a wall in the Juna Mahal at
Dungarpur. They are set against a background of scrolling stems
with flowers and enclosed within a narrow cusped frame.
Surrounding this are larger scale swirling stems and flowers, and a
further pair of birds. The composition in mirror- and coloured
glass is dazzling in both design and technique.

opposite Drawing based on the element above the circular mirror,
expanded at the bottom to make a complete design.

overleaf Drawing of an ambitious panel of polychrome glass mosaic
in the private apartments. A pair of chalice-like drinking vessels flank
a lidded urn on a table which has a beaded border and chevron side.
On either side are wine flasks and stylized peacocks.
All is set in a sea of leafed stems which loop back and
forth, ending with bold flowers.

opposite, above Painted decoration with a European flavour in a small
room that overlooks the Durbar Hall of Samode Palace (see p. 128).

opposite, below Looking from one end of the Sultan Mahal in
the palace through a screen of shallow cusped arches. Above the arches
are wide scenes of trays with fruit and flowers (*overleaf*), and in the
coving dark cartouches against a white background.

above This composition in an anteroom to the Shish Mahal
flanking the Durbar Hall shows even more European influence, in
the shapes of the urns and the elaborate scrollwork at the bottom. The
birds, however, are an Indian feature found throughout the palace.

overleaf Drawing of one of the panoramic scenes at the top of
the screen wall in the Sultan Mahal (*opposite, below*). The long narrow
format is unusual, but all the traditional elements are present.

As the royal princes travelled to Europe increasingly often
they were inspired by what they saw there, as their forebears had been
when they visited the Mughal court in Agra and Delhi. This
painted decoration in Samode Palace is even more European in
character than that seen earlier (pp. 230–31).

opposite Drawing based on the central panel, combined with the
outermost spandrels. The plain oval frame is a foreign import,
as are the shapes of the scrolls. But the birds and flower shapes show
that European influence has been adapted, rather
than straightforwardly adopted.

opposite Even in this small detail of the corridor round the upper level of the Durbar Hall in Samode Palace fauna abounds in the form of insects and birds, including a tiny owl standing on one leg. Here the style of the painting is entirely traditional.

right A blind arch in the Shish Mahal of Samode Palace. Whereas a similar composition in carved stone at Jaisalmer was filled with elaborate floral motifs (p. 204), here the craftsmen used an abstract grid of convex pieces of mirror glass. The dado is painted with two oval flowering shrubs surrounded by birds.

These murals in the Sultan Mahal in Samode Palace have the same
theme, a plant or tree formed into a circular shape, with variations.

above Here the tree is turquoise and its flowers, unusually, almost
black, but against the light background their dark tones leap out.

opposite, above A solid, dark tree is framed by two upstanding cypresses.
The background is rich with birds including peacock, parakeet, dove,
bulbul, and the migratory winter hoopoe.

opposite, below The circular shape of the symmetrical central motif
here is emphasized by the space that encloses it like a border.

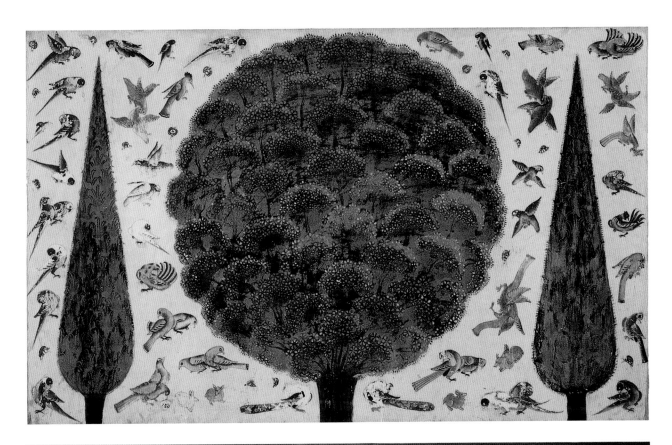

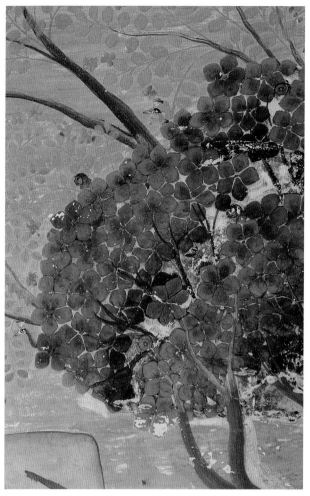

Details of two wall paintings in the
City Palace at Udaipur (*above and above right*) and
one in the Lake Palace there (*right*). Essentially
all three are pictorial scenes rather than
graphic designs. There is a considerable
difference in age between the early paintings
in the City Palace and the 19th-century one
in the Lake Palace, but the preoccupation
with the natural world, and the psychological
effect, are as strong.

opposite Drawing of a mango tree in blossom.
The design was recently created in marble
on a wall in Devi Garh Fort Palace, north
of Udaipur. In style it is close to the wall-
painting at Udaipur carried out generations
ago (*above*).

The decoration of the Chhavi Niwas complex, on the fifth floor of the Chandra Mahal in the City Palace at Jaipur, is an exuberant celebration of floral motifs. The use of just two colours, blue and white, creates a cool, refreshing environment, ideal for the torpid summer months. In earlier times this tone of blue would not have been easy to make, when Indian artists had to rely on turquoise and indigo. In the 19th century, however, new industrially produced colours were imported from Germany and Britain.

above The central space seen through the elegantly tapered columns and arches glows with light from windows on both sides.

above left, and opposite The dado has black borders which give weight to the lower part of the wall. The wider panels have tripartite designs of plants, a larger one flanked by two smaller narrow ones, with a creeper-like fluidity. In the wall above, a luxuriant design surrounds a convex central shape (see also pp. 244–45).

left A detail of the ceiling. Here the scrolling pattern has a character derived from the European Renaissance rather than India.

The central room of the Chhavi Niwas in the City Palace at Jaipur
(pp. 242–43) has openings in its thick walls that are rendered light
and energetic through the use of bold, large-scale
spiralling vegetation on the soffits of the arches. The dados
have plant motifs, and the upper walls between the windows
have arched compositions where the vegetation spreads out
and up and dances round an oval (*opposite*).

The Kuchaman Fort in Rajasthan has been in the hands of the same family since the early 1700s. They were closely associated with the Mughals in Agra, and their palace reflects this in its architecture and ornamentation. The Sunehri Burj or Chamber of Gold is a small room exquisitely decorated with a combination of painting on plaster and gilded gesso work that is as fine as that of the Anup Mahal in the Junagarh Fort at Bikaner (p. 188 and pp. 248–51) but not as profuse.

above left A detail of the floral painting on a wall.

above Gilded gesso ornament in a corner of the room. In the panel on the left, a vase flanked by two parakeets supports a pot from which a double spray of flowers and foliage springs forth (*opposite*).

left A detail of the ceiling, where a strong, elaborate trellis runs over a delicate grid of slender stems.

opposite The pattern executed in gilded gesso in the left-hand panel in the corner of the room (*above*).

The Anup Mahal in the Junagarh Fort at
Bikaner envelops the visitor with its oxblood-
coloured walls exquisitely covered in intricate
floral motifs in sculptured gesso covered
with gold leaf, and mirrors set in recessed
panels (see also p. 188 and pp. 250–51).
To the foreigner, it is the realization of
the most exotic room in one of the tales of
the Arabian Nights.

opposite, above left The Karan Mahal Chowk, largest of the many
courtyards of the Junagarh Fort at Bikaner, was built by
Maharaja Karan Singh in the late 17th century after his defeat of
the Mughal Emperor Aurangzeb.

above and opposite, below left Energetic scrolls and densely packed
stylized leaf and flower motifs in gilt gesso in a shallow niche in
the Anup Mahal (see also p. 248). The gilded ornament
round the mirror is itself set off by mirror glass.

opposite, below right The Gaj Mandir was the private apartment of the
18th-century ruler Maharaja Gaj Singh and his queens. Its walls have
delicate decoration of flowers and fruit and mirror glass.

opposite, above right The Gaj Mandir is surrounded by a passage with
jalis filled with coloured glass.

Ornamental Scenes | 251

above, and opposite, above left An image of a Hindu deity in
Samode Palace, realized in stained glass and seen in a drawing.

opposite, above right A *jali* in the City Palace at Udaipur. A composition
of squares that recalls the 16th-century Sidi Sayyid Mosque in
Ahmedabad (p. 208) is filled with multi-coloured stained glass.

opposite, below left and right The extraordinary Shish Mahal in Deogarh
Palace has windows with plain coloured glass. Elsewhere in the palace,
stained glass fills a *jali* with hexagons and stars.

ACKNOWLEDGMENTS

A lot of travelling took place to cover the various locations included in this book, by car, train, plane, auto-rickshaw and bicycle. As ever it was an extraordinary experience, from the exemplary monuments to the *chai-wallas*. *Chai* – tea – is my particular predilection, with or without ginger or cardamon. Along the way I met so many people, fell into so many conversations with strangers, had so many questions answered, encountered so much warmth and good will. I should like to thank all those many, many people who were unfailingly as helpful as they could be to a foreigner in their country who had stubbornly refused to learn their language.

There are a number of people I would like to thank particularly, not only because they have given me so much moral support and real friendship but because they have often tried to 'push' me, determined that I should work hard towards my goals, making me more ambitious than I naturally would be, opening up further possibilities, who when motivation or spirit flagged have been there to give me mental sustenance.

For their warm friendship and generosity I thank Yuvraj Harshvardan Singh and Yuvrani Priyadarshani Kumari of Dungarpur, who between them have worked so hard over many years to make Udai Bilas Palace a home for its many guests. It is one of my favourite places in India. I should like to thank Bronwyn Latif and her husband, Salim. Bronwyn is a human *tour de force* with wonderful creative talent; she is also remarkably generous, never hesitating to pick up the telephone to create a contact for me. To me she is fearless. Thank you very much, Bronwyn. For her dry wit, conversation and love I want to thank Jaya Wheaton. Downcast or confused, after spending time with Jaya I always sleep easy at night. From the bottom of my heart, I thank you. Thanks to Christopher Moore for doing what he has done, creating a successful textile business, often in difficult circumstances. You are an inspiration. To M. K. Daivat Singh of Sirohi and his wife Kirti Kumari and daughter Yogini Kumari, thank you for all your warm affection and steadfastness – Kirti, I wonder about 'past lives'? And thanks to Gautam Mukerjee for his warm friendship, generous hospitality and dry wit.

Back home in London, I am deeply grateful to Shauna Dennison and Carley Bean for looking after me so generously, making work a sheer pleasure. More *karaoke* please! I should also like to thank Helen Ball for her support, belief in me, constant encouragement. I am indebted to Rupert Thomas for giving my work a chance to breathe, and cheering me with 'Enough of being nervous, Henry.' Thanks to Dr John Snelson. Nothing can detract from a very happy past. And to Jenny Mauther: I have never forgotten all the real affection, companionship and generosity – I understand now, *mea culpa*. I would like to thank Maria Lord for pre-editing all my text, undaunted: another Indophile, your knowledge and experience have been invaluable and your friendship greatly appreciated. Thank you to my Mother and Father: the way they brought me up made me what I am today – none of this would have been possible without their ongoing support and help.

For their generous cooperation in facilitating my work, my thanks go to the Mehrengarh Fort Trust, Jodhpur, Rajasthan; the Samode Hotels, Jaipur, Rajasthan, and Bandhavgarh, Madhya Pradesh; and the Maharana Mewar Charitable Foundation, Udaipur, Rajasthan.

Lastly I would like to express my great admiration for the many, many thousands of men and women up and down the width and breadth of the subcontinent who are keeping their crafts alive today despite the massive cultural change that India is undergoing – and for all those visionary people who are determined to ensure that these noble men and women have relevance and a market in a fast-changing society.

BIBLIOGRAPHY

James H. Bae *In a World of Gods and Goddesses: The Mystic Art of Indra Sharma*, San Rafael, Calif., 2003

Michael Barry *Colour and Symbolism in Islamic Architecture*, London and New York 1996

Enakshi Bhavnani *Decorative Designs on Stone and Wood in India*, Bombay 1978

Percy Brown *Indian Architecture (Islamic Period)*, 5th edn, Bombay 1968

– *Indian Architecture (Buddhist and Hindu Periods)*, 7th repr., Bombay 1976

Dominique Clevenot and Gerard Degeorge *Ornament and Decoration in Islamic Architecture*, London and New York 2000

Roy C. Craven *A Concise History of Indian Art*, London and New York 1976

Richard Grimmett and Tim Inskipp *Birds of Northern India*, London 2003

Issam El-Said and Ayse Parman *Geometric Concepts in Islamic Art*, London 1976

John Keay *India Discovered*, Leicester 1981

Ebba Koch *The Complete Taj Mahal*, London and New York 2006

George Michell *The Majesty of Mughal Decoration: The Art and Architecture of Islamic India*, London and New York 2007

– (photographs by Antonio Martinelli) *The Royal Palaces of India*, London and New York 1994

– *Palaces of Rajasthan*, Bombay 2004

Aman Nath *Jaipur: The Last Destination*, Bombay 1993

– and Francis Wacziag *Arts and Crafts of Rajasthan*, London and New York 1987

Naveen Patnaik *The Garden of Life: an Introduction to the Healing Plants of India*, London 1993

Yves Porter and Gerard Degeorge *The Glory of the Sultans (Islamic Architecture in India)*, Paris 2009

V. S. Pramar *Haveli (Wooden Houses and Mansions of Gujarat)*, Ahmedabad 1989

Aditi Ranjan and M. P. Ranjan, eds *Handmade in India (Crafts of India)*, New Delhi 2007

L. F. Rushbrook Williams, ed. *Murray's Handbook for Travellers in India, Pakistan, Burma and Ceylon*, 21st edn, London 1968

Mira Seth *Indian Painting (The Great Mural Tradition)*, New York 2006

Kireet Patel, Reena Shah and Reenal Agarwal *Arayish (Wall Paintings of Shekhawati)*, Ahmedabad 2006

Christopher Tadgell *The History of Architecture in India*, London 1990

Jay Thakkar *Naqsh (The Art of Wood Carving in Traditional Houses of Gujarat: A Focus on Ornamentation)*, Ahmedabad 2004

G. H. R. Tillotson *Mughal India*, London and San Francisco 1990

– *The Rajput Palaces: The Development of an Architectural Style, 1450–1750*, Oxford and New Delhi 1999

INDEX

Photographer, artist and writer Henry Wilson has long been a lover of India,
and has travelled there extensively. His first book was *Benares*, published
by Thames & Hudson in 1985. Since then his photographs have appeared in
The World of Interiors, *Architectural Digest* and other magazines, and in books, most
recently *India Contemporary* (2007), also published by Thames & Hudson.
His drawings of motifs from Indian architecture, as seen in the
present book, inspired Osborne & Little to commission
the Sariskar Collection of wallpapers from him.
Photograph by Shauna Dennison